ESSENTIAL MORMON
Celebrations

ESSENTIAL MORMON

Celebrations

Secret Combinations for Holidays,
Homecomings, Potluck Dinners, and More

JULIE BADGER JENSEN

DESERET
BOOK

Salt Lake City, Utah

Visit us at deseretbook.com

Library of Congress Cataloging-in-Publication Data

Jensen, Julie Badger.
  Essential Mormon celebrations / Julie Badger Jensen.
      p.   cm.
  Includes index.
  ISBN 1-59038-478-4 (spiral bound)
  1. Holiday cookery. 2. Cookery, Mormon. 3. Menus. I. Title.
  TX739.J46 2005
  641.5'68—dc22   2005017926

Printed in Canada   29359
Friesens, Manitoba, Canada

10   9   8   7   6   5   4   3   2   1

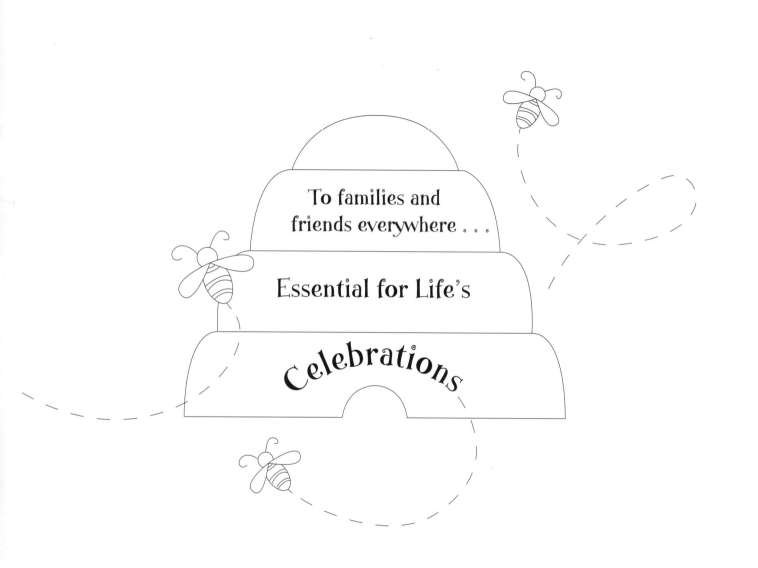

To families and
friends everywhere . . .

Essential for Life's

Celebrations

This is the day which the Lord hath made; we will rejoice and be glad in it.

—Psalm 118:24

CONTENTS

INTRODUCTION

We all love celebrations—sharing happy times with family, friends, neighbors, and community. We relish the biblical advice, "Rejoice together" (John 4:36). Throughout the year, numerous holidays, family events, and other occasions call for rejoicing. And a big part of every celebration is food.

In winter, sweet smells and festive foods brighten the cold days as we anticipate cozy Christmas Eves and merry Christmas mornings.

In spring, we celebrate glorious Easter and find wonder in the earth as it comes to life . . . nodding tulips, lavender lilacs, and happy laughter. We savor the heavenly aroma of hot rolls and glazed ham.

Summer is splashed with golden sunshine, afternoon swims, hikes by mountain streams, sizzling barbecues, pioneer picnics, and fireworks. We enjoy dear neighbors, happy graduations, patriotic parades, Church potlucks, and heartfelt homecomings.

Then, in autumn, peace is found in home and harvest and gratitude felt as heads bow together around the Thanksgiving table.

Timeless traditions, great gatherings, and happy holidays become a precious part of living as we "rejoice together."

Written to bring cheer, this book is meant to encourage joyful gatherings. I hope the treasured recipes and well-loved menus within the pages of this book will be useful in planning and enjoying celebrations.

Warm appreciation is expressed to the great Deseret Book team, especially Sheri Dew, Jana Erickson, Tony Benjamin, Jack Lyon, Lisa Mangum, Laurie Cook, and Angie Godfrey. Special thanks to Sheryl Smith for cover design and artwork and Janna DeVore for editing and indexing the book. My gratitude goes to Stephanie and Christopher Dansie, our daughter and her husband, for cheerful technical assistance, and to my darling mother for a lifetime of happy celebrations. Heartfelt thanks to my loving husband and cherished family for priceless encouragement and help in many ways.

WINTER

THE NIGHT BEFORE CHRISTMAS

Softly falling snow is seen through frosty panes, and the fragrance of cinnamon and peppermint is all through the house. A crackling fire warms hearts as families and friends gather on Christmas Eve.

Whether celebrating with old traditions or beginning new ones, you can feel the joy of priceless time together with those you love. The following menu is warm and festive, full of flavor, yet simple. The aroma of Honey-Glazed Ham and Creamy Potato Soup fills the kitchen as family arrives. Crisp, red apples, sparkling pomegranate, and the crunch of candied walnuts add to the spirit. Choose from two beautiful holiday desserts: rich vanilla ice cream "Snowballs" glowing with red candles or Angel Food Cake with peppermint cream and Chocolate Sauce.

Gather around the table and feel the warmth. Perhaps there will be candlelight conversations of that first Christmas long ago as children's eyes sparkle with wonder. Cherish the moments on that beautiful eve—the night before Christmas—and reflect on the life of our Lord.

Honey-Glazed Ham and Buns

The sweet smells of Christmas float "all through the house."

1   4–pound precooked ham, thinly sliced
½   cup honey
2   teaspoons mustard
½   teaspoon ground cloves
2   teaspoons Worcestershire sauce
12   large buns

Place ham in roasting pan. In a separate bowl, stir together honey, mustard, cloves, and Worcestershire sauce. Spoon sauce over surface of the ham. Bake at 325 degrees for about 30 minutes or until warmed through. Makes enough meat for about 12 large sandwiches.

Creamy Potato Soup

This savory soup warms the winter night.

12   medium potatoes
1   cup chopped onion
¼   cup butter or margarine
2   cups cream
3   cups milk
1   tablespoon salt
2   cups grated cheddar cheese
4   green onions, finely sliced
1   pound bacon, fried crisp, drained, and crumbled
    Salt and pepper to taste

Peel and quarter potatoes and place in a large pot. Fill pot with water just to cover potatoes. Put on lid; bring to a boil. Reduce heat to medium and cook for 30 minutes or until tender. Place chopped onions and butter or margarine in a microwave-safe bowl and heat on high power for 2 minutes; set aside. Remove potatoes from heat and drain. Add cream; stir together. Mash potatoes until mixture is smooth. Stir in milk, salt, and onion-butter mixture. Return pot to stove and simmer over low heat for about 10 minutes, stirring occasionally. Watch carefully to avoid scorching. Turn down heat if necessary. Pass cheese, green onions, and bacon for topping individual servings. Salt and pepper to taste. Makes about 12 cups.

THE NIGHT BEFORE CHRISTMAS

Red-Apple Walnut Salad

This salad is crisp and crunchy.

4 **red apples, coarsely chopped**

¼ **cup orange juice**

2 **(16–ounce) bags mixed salad greens**

1 **(6-ounce) carton Gorgonzola cheese (optional)**

¾ **cup pomegranate seeds or Craisins®**

1 **recipe Candied Walnuts (see next column)**

1 **recipe Winter Salad Dressing (see next column)**

One half hour before serving time, combine apples and orange juice to keep apples fresh. At serving time, drain off juices. Place salad greens, apples, Gorgonzola cheese, pomegranate seeds or Craisins, and candied walnuts in a large bowl and toss lightly. Toss with desired amount of Winter Salad Dressing or pass dressing for individual servings. Makes 8 servings.

Note: To remove pomegranate seeds, cut pomegranate into four sections. Fill a large bowl half full of water. Place one section at a time under water. With fingers, release the seeds. When seeds from all four sections have been released, empty the bowl into a colander to drain. Remove any white pith. This method prevents splattering and staining and can be done a day in advance.

CANDIED WALNUTS

½ **cup sugar**

2 **tablespoons water**

1 **cup walnuts**

Line a baking sheet with well-greased foil or parchment paper. Place sugar and water in a small saucepan; stir to moisten sugar evenly. Bring to a simmer over medium heat and cook and stir until sugar melts and caramelizes to a rich amber-brown color; watch carefully to avoid scorching. Remove from heat. Add walnuts and stir with a fork to coat nuts. Place nuts on baking sheet, separating nuts with the fork into an even layer. Let cool until caramel hardens. Can be made several days ahead.

WINTER SALAD DRESSING

½ **cup red wine vinegar**

½ **cup vegetable oil or olive oil**

1 **teaspoon salt**

1 **teaspoon ground pepper**

1 **clove garlic, minced**

½ **cup honey**

In a 1-quart jar, combine all dressing ingredients; shake vigorously. Refrigerate at least 4 hours. Dressing can be made a week in advance. Makes about 2 cups.

Snowballs

These snowballs will light up the night with merriment.

- 1 (14-ounce) bag flaked coconut
- ½ gallon carton vanilla ice cream
- 1 recipe Chocolate Sauce (see next column)

  Small candles, for garnish

  Sprigs of holly, for garnish

Place coconut in a shallow bowl. Remove ice cream from freezer and thaw at room temperature for about 10 minutes. Peel carton from ice cream. With a knife, cut ice cream in half and then in fourths, making 8 slices. Quickly shape each slice into a ball and roll in coconut. Place Snowballs on a tray. Freeze until very hard. On day of serving, place individual serving bowls in freezer to chill. At serving time, remove bowls from freezer. Place about 2 tablespoons Chocolate Sauce in bottom of each bowl. Remove Snowballs from freezer. Place one Snowball in each frosty bowl. Place a small candle in each. Light candles and serve with a sprig of holly if desired. Makes 8 Snowballs.

Quick Peppermint-Stick Cake

Have a holly jolly Christmas.

- 2 cups whipping cream, plus sugar to sweeten
- 2 peppermint sticks or candy canes, crushed
- 2 drops red food coloring
- 1 large angel food cake
- 10 small candy canes

  Sprigs of holly, for garnish
- 1 recipe Chocolate Sauce (see below)

Whip cream until stiff, adding sugar to sweeten. Stir in crushed peppermint sticks and red food coloring. Slice cake into three layers. Spread flavored whipped cream in between each layer and on top and sides of cake. Garnish individual servings with a small candy cane and holly, if desired. Pass Chocolate Sauce for topping. Makes 10 servings.

CHOCOLATE SAUCE

- 1 (14-ounce) can Eagle Brand® sweetened condensed milk
- 1 (1-ounce) square unsweetened chocolate
- 1 tablespoon vanilla

Place sweetened condensed milk and chocolate square in a microwave-safe bowl and cook on high power for two minutes. Remove from microwave. Add vanilla and beat with hand mixer until smooth. Refrigerate sauce until cooled to desired temperature. Mixture will thicken as it cools. Sauce can be made ahead and reheated.

A MERRY CHRISTMAS DINNER

A glowing tree, blazing fire, loving gifts, happy children, and merry hearts all add to the joy of Christmas. Luke 15:32 reminds us, "We should make merry, and be glad."

There is nothing more merry—or loving and traditional—to share at Christmas than a dinner. A glorious meal can be a marvelous blending of old and new favorites. If you're looking for a delicious menu that is easy to prepare, consider the recipes that follow. As an entrée for your Christmas dinner, choose the Festive Beef Rib Roast and Baked Potatoes with Topping or a simple but tasty dish of Cubed Beef with Gravy served over Holiday Rice. Both are wonderful with piping-hot Popovers, Snap Peas and Cherry Tomatoes, and Sparkling Citrus Salad. The grand finale, Old English Trifle, takes some time but is beautiful. Children can help make it the day before.

This time together is precious. Let the light of the season burn brightly as loved ones gather around the table in a spirit of gratitude and love for the birth and life of the Savior.

Festive Beef Rib Roast

A roast destined to be the majestic star of the feast!

- 1 6- to 7-pound standing rib roast of beef
  Salt

  Pepper
- 1 recipe Herb Rub (optional) (see below)
  Fresh parsley for garnishing
- 1 recipe Horseradish Sauce (see next column)

Salt and pepper roast. Spread Herb Rub over top and sides of roast, if desired. Insert meat thermometer so tip is in center of thickest part of beef and does not touch bone. Roast at 325 degrees for about 2½ to 3 hours to desired doneness. Meat thermometer will read 140 degrees for rare roast, 160 degrees for medium, and 170 degrees for well-done beef. Remove roast from oven. Place loose foil tent over roast and let stand for 15 minutes before carving. Place on serving platter. Garnish with fresh parsley. Serve with Horseradish Sauce, if desired. Makes about 12 servings.

HERB RUB

- ¾ cup chopped fresh parsley
- 2 tablespoons chopped fresh thyme or 2 teaspoons dried
- 1 tablespoon olive or vegetable oil
- 2 cloves garlic, finely chopped

Mix all ingredients. Refrigerate at least one hour to blend flavors. Rub over top and sides of any beef roast before roasting.

HORSERADISH SAUCE

- 1 cup sour cream
- 1 tablespoon horseradish sauce
- ¼ teaspoon pepper

Stir ingredients together. Serve with roast.

Baked Potatoes with Topping

What a great blend of flavors!

- 2 cups grated cheddar cheese
- 1 cup sour cream
- ½ teaspoon salt
- 8 potatoes
- ¼ cup finely sliced green onion
- 8 slices bacon, cooked and crumbled (optional)

Stir together cheddar cheese, sour cream, and salt; refrigerate until ready to serve. Wrap potatoes in foil and place on a baking sheet. Bake at 400 degrees for about 1 hour and 15 minutes or until tender. When ready to serve, remove foil from potatoes. Slit each potato. Place potatoes on serving platter. Top with sour cream and cheese mixture. Garnish with green onions and bacon, if desired. Makes 8 potatoes and topping.

Cubed Beef with Gravy

Simply delicious!

- 4 **pounds stewing beef**
- 2 **(1-ounce) packages dry onion soup mix**
- 2 **large (26-ounce) cans cream of mushroom soup**
- 2 **(8-ounce) cans mushrooms (optional)**
  Sour cream, for topping

Place stewing beef in a Dutch oven or other heavy baking dish. Sprinkle with dry onion soup mix. Spoon mushroom soup over top. Cover with lid or tight foil. Bake in oven at 325 degrees for about 3 hours. Stir in mushrooms, if desired, during last 30 minutes of baking. Pass sour cream for topping individual servings. Serve over Holiday Rice. Makes 8 to 10 servings.

Holiday Rice

This dish is sprinkled with holiday cheer.

- ½ **cup chopped onion**
- ¼ **cup butter**
- 3 **cups uncooked instant rice**
- 3 **cups water**
- ½ **teaspoon salt**
- 2 **tablespoons chopped parsley**
- 1 **tomato, chopped**

In a large saucepan, sauté onion in butter over medium-high heat. Add rice and heat until golden. Stir in water and salt. Bring to a boil and cook for 5 minutes over medium heat. Remove from heat. Cover and let stand for 20 minutes or until water is absorbed into rice. Place in serving bowl. Just before serving, sprinkle parsley and chopped tomatoes over rice. Makes 8 to 10 servings.

Popovers

These "high-hat" muffins are spectacular and simple. Just pop them in the oven.

- 2 **cups flour**
- ½ **teaspoon salt**
- 4 **eggs, lightly beaten**
- 2 **cups milk**
- 1 **tablespoon butter, melted**

In a medium bowl, sift together flour and salt; set aside. Place eggs, milk, and butter in a blender and blend briefly. Add dry ingredients and blend until smooth. Pour into 12 well-greased muffin cups. Bake at 400 degrees for 20 to 25 minutes, until popovers raise high and are lightly browned. Serve hot with butter and jam. May be cooled, frozen, and later reheated at 350 degrees for 5 to 10 minutes. Makes 12 popovers.

Snap Peas and Cherry Tomatoes

Red and green proclaim the season.

4   **cups frozen sugar snap peas**
1   **pound cherry or grape tomatoes**
     Butter, to taste
     Salt, to taste

Place 2 inches of water in a large saucepan. Bring water to a boil. Add peas; bring to a second boil. Reduce heat to low and simmer for about 5 minutes. Lightly butter and salt to taste. Just before serving, toss with tomatoes. Makes 8 to 10 servings.

Sparkling Citrus Salad

This jeweled fruit platter is sure to make spirits bright.

4   **grapefruit**
4   **kiwifruit**
4   **red apples**
2   **ripe avocados**
     Red leaf lettuce
     Powdered sugar
2   **large (15-ounce) cans mandarin oranges, drained**
1   **cup pomegranate seeds or Craisins®**

Prepare grapefruit by peeling off skin, including the pith, and then carefully cutting between membranes of each section, removing one grapefruit section at a time. Reserve grapefruit juice; place sections in juice and refrigerate until time to serve. This can be done a day in advance.

An hour before serving time, cut kiwifruit into thick slices—about four slices per kiwi. Slice apples. Peel and slice avocados. Spoon reserved grapefruit juice over apples and avocados; stir to coat. This will keep them looking fresh. Remove grapefruit sections from juice and place, with the apple slices, on a platter lined with red leaf lettuce. Sprinkle lightly with powdered sugar. Top with kiwifruit and avocado slices, mandarin oranges, and pomegranate seeds. Makes 8 to 10 servings.

Note: To remove pomegranate seeds, cut pomegranate into four sections. Fill a large bowl half full of water. Place one section at a time under water. With fingers, release the seeds. When seeds from all four sections have been released, empty the bowl into a colander to drain. Remove any white pith. This method prevents splattering and staining and can be done a day in advance.

Old English Trifle

A fabulous finale to the feast!

- 1 **yellow cake mix and ingredients as listed on package**
- 1 **large (6-ounce) package strawberry Jell-O®**
- 2 **cups boiling water**
- 1 **(16-ounce) package frozen strawberries, semi-thawed**
- 2 **cups fresh strawberries, sliced**
- 1 **large (6-ounce) package vanilla instant pudding**
- 2 **cups milk**
- 1 **cup whipping cream**
- 2 **tablespoons sugar**

First Layer: Prepare cake mix as directed on package. Bake in 2 well-greased round baking pans. After cake is cooled, break one round of cake into 2- to 3-inch pieces. (Reserve other cake round for another purpose or a second trifle.) Place cake pieces in the bottom of large glass compote or bowl. In a saucepan, dissolve strawberry Jell-O in 2 cups boiling water. Cool. Refrigerate until thick and syrupy. Stir in semi-thawed strawberries. Pour over cake pieces. Refrigerate for about 1 hour or until firm. Cover with fresh strawberry slices.

Second Layer: Prepare vanilla pudding according to package directions, but using only 2 cups of milk. Pour over strawberry Jell-O and sliced strawberries. Refrigerate for 30 minutes or until firm.

Third Layer: Whip cream until stiff. Stir in sugar. Spread over top of first two layers. Makes 8 to 10 servings.

NEW YEAR'S EVE

There are many ways to celebrate New Year's Eve. Let your creativity abound as you dream up ideas to celebrate. Here are just a few: plan a casual family supper with games and puzzles; host an open house; enjoy a cozy dinner for two. The options and themes really are endless. And one thing is sure: everyone will look forward to the food and fun you have planned. If children make it till the midnight hour, let them add to the excitement with their enthusiasm for party hats, horns, and noise as the clock strikes twelve.

After all the holiday party food of the past weeks, your guests will appreciate a change in cuisine. The menu that follows is full of Asian-themed food and may be just what you've been craving. Check out other recipes in the book for even more ideas (Sweet-and-Sour Pork on page 77 or Polynesian Chicken Salad on page 78, for example). Wrap up your celebration with some refreshing Orange Blossom Ice and homemade Fortune Cookies, prepared to symbolize good luck and prosperity for the coming year. Let New Year's Eve be a time to rejoice, a time to glance back and move forward with optimism, a time to "be of good cheer" (John 16:33).

Sesame Chicken Wraps

Rolled in a lettuce leaf, these are fun to eat!

4   **tablespoons soy sauce**
4   **tablespoons brown sugar**
1   **tablespoon cornstarch**
2   **cups chicken breast strips**
1   **tablespoon butter**
4   **tablespoons sesame seeds**
2   **tablespoons sesame oil**
6   **butter lettuce leaves**

Combine soy sauce, brown sugar, and cornstarch in a small bowl; pour over chicken strips and stir to coat. Set aside for 15 minutes. In a frying pan, melt butter over low heat. Add sesame seeds and cook until lightly browned. Set aside to cool. In a separate skillet, heat sesame oil over medium heat. Quickly stir-fry the chicken in the heated oil just until cooked through. Combine sesame seeds with chicken. Spoon one-sixth of the mixture atop the center of each lettuce leaf. Fold lettuce into a wrap to be eaten by hand. Place on a platter. Makes 6 sesame chicken bundles.

Beef and Broccoli

This dish may become a tradition.

1   **pound top round beef steak**
¼   **cup soy sauce**
2   **tablespoons sugar**
¼   **cup white grape juice or apple juice**
2   **tablespoons cornstarch**
1   **cup water**
2   **cups fresh broccoli florets, stems removed**
4   **tablespoons vegetable or olive oil, divided**
2   **cloves garlic, minced**
2   **teaspoons sesame oil**

Cut beef steak into 2-inch strips; set aside. Combine soy sauce, sugar, juice, cornstarch, and water in a small bowl; set aside. In a large skillet, stir-fry broccoli in 2 tablespoons oil for about 5 minutes over medium heat. Do not overcook. Place broccoli in another dish. Pour remaining oil in the same skillet and heat on medium-high heat. Add beef steak and cook until well browned on all sides, about 10 minutes. Add garlic and cook until fragrant, not more than 1 minute. Pour soy sauce mixture over meat and cook until slightly thickened. Stir in sesame oil. Remove from heat. Stir in broccoli. Serve over hot steamed rice. Makes 8 servings.

Chinese Vegetables

A welcome change.

- 1 **bunch celery, cut diagonally in 1-inch slices (about 4 cups)**
- 2 **cups water**
- ½ **onion, sliced in rings**
- ¼ **cup butter**
- 8 **ounces fresh mushrooms, sliced**
- 1 **(7-ounce) can sliced water chestnuts, drained**
- 1 **(10-ounce) can cream of chicken soup**
- 1 **teaspoon salt**
- 1 **(9.5-ounce) can chow mein noodles**
- ½ **cup slivered almonds, toasted**

In a saucepan, cook celery in water until tender, about 10 minutes; drain and set aside. Cook and stir onion rings in butter over medium heat until golden. Add mushrooms and cook for about 5 minutes more. Combine celery, onion, mushrooms, and water chestnuts with cream of chicken soup in a greased 1½- to 2-quart casserole dish and bake at 350 degrees for about 30 minutes. Serve over chow mein noodles. Top with toasted almonds. Makes 6 to 8 servings.

Jasmine Rice

This flavorful rice is available at supermarkets.

- 1 **cup chopped onion**
- ¼ **cup olive oil or butter**
- 2 **cloves garlic, minced**
- 2 **(10-ounce) cans beef consommé soup**
- ½ **teaspoon salt**
- ½ **cup water**
- 1 **teaspoon cinnamon (optional)**
- 2 **cups jasmine rice**
- ½ **cup currants or Craisins®**
- ½ **cup pine nuts or slivered almonds**
- 1 **tablespoon olive oil**
- 2 **tablespoons chopped fresh parsley**

In a large pan, briefly sauté onions in 4 tablespoons olive oil or butter. Add garlic and sauté for one more minute. Add beef consommé soup, salt, water, and cinnamon and bring to a boil. Stir in jasmine rice; cover. Reduce heat to low and simmer for 20 minutes or until moisture is absorbed. Add currants or Craisins. In a small pan, sauté pine nuts or slivered almonds in 1 tablespoon olive oil over low heat for about 1 minute until lightly browned. Just before serving, add pine nuts or almonds and fresh parsley to rice. Makes 8 to 10 servings.

Orange Blossom Ice

Delight in the frosty citrus flavor of this treat.

4 **cups sugar**
4 **cups water**
4 **cups orange juice**
Juice from 2 lemons
1 **teaspoon almond or vanilla extract**

In a large saucepan, bring sugar and water to a boil. Reduce heat to low and simmer for about 5 minutes to dissolve sugar. Cool. Combine with orange and lemon juice. Stir in almond or vanilla extract. Place in a container and freeze overnight. Remove from freezer just before serving. Spoon into small bowls or glasses. Garnish with an edible flower if desired. Makes about 6 cups.

Fortune Cookies

The future is looking good!

3 **egg whites**
½ **cup white sugar**
¼ **cup brown sugar**
½ **cup flour**
½ **teaspoon vanilla**

Prepare 12 fortunes on thin strips of paper and have ready to place in cookies. Place all ingredients in a blender. Mix for about 5 seconds. Cover cookie sheets with greased parchment paper. Drop dough by measured tablespoons onto cookie sheets (only 4 per sheet). Bake at 350 degrees for about 8 minutes. Immediately remove cookies from cookie sheet with spatula and place on a flat surface. Put a fortune in the middle of each cookie. Fold cookie in half (the rough side should be on the inside). Bring corners up to form fortune cookie shape. Let oven cool to 200 degrees. Put all the finished cookies back on the cookie sheet and bake until completely browned, about 30 minutes. Have fun being creative with fortunes. The cookies may look a little homemade, but that's part of the charm. Makes 12 cookies.

SIMPLE NEW YEAR'S DAY BRUNCH

When New Year's Day arrives, it's time to relax. A brunch may be just what you've been wishing for—informal entertaining at its best. This menu is sure to brighten the day for everyone and echo the sentiment of the Psalmist: "Joy cometh in the morning" (Psalm 30:5). Let family and friends join in the fun by preparing this easy and delicious meal together. You may want to tell them in advance of your plan and have ready additional copies of the recipes for each person to work from.

Those first to arrive could section grapefruit after reading directions from the Sparkling Citrus Salad recipe on page 11 of this book. Someone could prepare the Holiday Hot Chocolate. Others could grate cheese, dice ham, and chop vegetables for the Quick Quiche. While it's baking, everyone can enjoy a cup of steaming hot chocolate.

When the quiche is ready, the Homestyle Baked Scones can go into the oven. By the time guests gather around the table, the scones should be ready to serve piping hot, along with the Ruby Grapefruit and hot chocolate refills. Everyone is bound to have a great time, and cooking brunch together might just become a new tradition.

Ruby Grapefruit

Beautiful!

- 4 **large grapefruit**
- 4 **tablespoons sugar**
- 1 **(10-ounce) package frozen raspberries with syrup**

Peel and section grapefruit. Sprinkle with sugar. Place in 8 small bowls. Thaw raspberries until frosty. Spoon raspberries and juice over grapefruit. Serve immediately. Makes 8 servings.

Quick Quiche

Simply delicious!

- 1 **(10-ounce) package frozen chopped spinach**
- 8 **eggs**
- 3 **cups milk**
- 1 **teaspoon salt**
- ½ **cup chopped onion**
- ½ **cup butter, melted**
- 1½ **cups Bisquick®**
- 2 **cups grated cheddar or Monterey Jack cheese**
- 2 **cups diced ham**
- 1 **recipe Quiche Sauce (see next column)**
  Parsley, chopped
- 1 **red pepper, diced, for garnish**

Prepare spinach according to package directions. Drain and squeeze out liquid; set aside. Beat eggs in a large bowl; stir in milk and salt. In a small bowl, microwave onion in butter for about 2 minutes; stir into egg mixture. Whisk in Bisquick. Add spinach, cheese, and ham. Pour into a greased 9x13-inch baking dish. Bake at 350 degrees for about 50 minutes or until cooked through. Let stand for 10 minutes before cutting into squares. Top each serving with Quiche Sauce. Garnish with parsley and red pepper. Makes about 12 servings.

QUICHE SAUCE

- 1 **(10-ounce) can cream of mushroom soup, undiluted**
- ½ **cup sour cream**

Place soup in a saucepan. Cook and stir over medium heat until hot. Remove from heat and stir in sour cream.

Homestyle Baked Scones

You'll love the homemade goodness of these scones.

- 3½ **cups flour**
- ½ **cup sugar**
- 1 **tablespoon baking powder**
- 1 **teaspoon salt**
- 3½ **cups whipping cream, divided**
- 1½ **cups cranberries**
- **Sugar for dipping**

In a bowl, combine flour, sugar, baking powder, and salt; stir well. Add 3 cups whipping cream, reserving ½ cup, and the cranberries; stir just until moist. Roll dough out on a floured surface. Using a round cookie cutter or a glass, cut dough into circles. Dip tops of unbaked scones in remaining whipping cream and then in sugar. Place on lightly greased cookie sheets (12 per sheet). Bake at 425 degrees for 12 to 14 minutes. Serve warm with butter. Makes about 30 scones.

Holiday Hot Chocolate

Enjoy an elegant cup of good cheer.

- 1 **cup sugar**
- ⅓ **cup Hershey's® unsweetened cocoa**
- ⅛ **teaspoon salt**
- 1 **cup water**
- 5½ **cups milk**
- 1 **(12-ounce) can evaporated milk or 1½ cups cream**
- 1 **tablespoon vanilla**

In a saucepan, combine sugar, cocoa, and salt; add water. Cook and stir over medium heat until mixture boils. Boil and stir 2 minutes. Stir in milk and evaporated milk or cream and heat. Do not boil. Remove from heat and add vanilla. Pour into a thermos for easy serving. Makes 8 cups.

SIMPLE NEW YEAR'S DAY BRUNCH

FOOTBALL FEVER FEST

A "Bowl Party" is a lot of fun. No matter what teams are playing or how little some of your guests know about the game, you can create an exciting party with fabulous and robust food. For your game plan, serve food in bowls or mugs; they are casual and easy to handle. Finger foods will also work well since most people want to sit or stand around the television screen.

Hearty Chili or smooth Cheese Soup are sure to be winners for the event. Nachos and dips are long-time favorites, and you're sure to hear cheers for Teriyaki Buffalo Wings and Sweet and Sour Meatballs. Have plenty of drinks and ice on hand. Score with marvelous Mud Pie Brownies. And, most important of all, have a ball as you enjoy this terrific tradition.

Hearty Chili

This is a winner!

1   pound ground beef

1   cup chopped onion

½   cup chopped red or green pepper (optional)

1   (28-ounce) can diced tomatoes

1   (30-ounce) can dark red kidney beans, undrained

1   (15-ounce) can chili

1   teaspoon salt

1   tablespoon chili powder

1   tablespoon sugar

2   cloves garlic, minced, or 1 teaspoon garlic salt

½   teaspoon pepper

½   cup ketchup

Brown ground beef in a large, heavy pan. Add onions and peppers and cook until tender. Add remaining ingredients and simmer uncovered over low heat for at least 1 hour. Chili can be made the day before and reheated. Makes about 8 cups.

Cheese Soup

Savor this smooth comfort food.

1   cup butter

1   cup flour

2   (14-ounce) cans chicken broth

4   cups milk

2   teaspoons salt

1   (15-ounce) jar Cheese Whiz®

3   carrots, sliced

3   stalks celery, sliced

1   medium onion, chopped

½   cup water

1   (10-ounce) package frozen green peas

Melt butter over medium heat in a large soup pot. Add flour and stir until smooth. Add chicken broth and milk and stir over medium heat until mixture comes to a boil. Continue stirring until thickened, about 2 minutes. Remove from heat. Add salt and Cheese Whiz and stir until well blended; set aside. In another saucepan, place carrots, celery, and onion in ½ cup water. Bring to a boil. Simmer for about 15 minutes or until vegetables are tender. Stir vegetables into cheese mixture. Just before serving, add frozen green peas and heat through briefly. Makes about 10 cups.

Touchdown Nachos

Score with this one!

1 **pound ground beef**
1 **(1.25-ounce) package taco seasoning**
½ **cup water**
1 **(16-ounce) can refried beans**
1 **bag (13½-ounce) tortilla chips**
4 **cups grated cheddar cheese**
4 **medium tomatoes, chopped**
2 **cups sour cream**
2 **cups salsa**

Brown ground beef in a large skillet. Add taco seasoning and water. Stir and cook over low heat for about 5 minutes. Stir in refried beans. Continue cooking until warmed through. Place tortilla chips in two greased 9x13-inch baking dishes. Drop the beef and bean mixture by tablespoons onto chips. Sprinkle with cheese. Bake at 450 degrees just until cheese is melted. Remove from oven. Sprinkle with tomatoes. Place sour cream and salsa in bowls for dipping. Makes about 16 servings.

Dilly Dip

This dip is great with crisp vegetables.

1 **cup sour cream**
1 **cup mayonnaise**
1 **tablespoon chopped fresh dill weed or 1 teaspoon dried dill weed**
1 **tablespoon chopped fresh parsley**
1 **green onion, chopped**
1 **teaspoon garlic salt**
1 **tablespoon fresh lemon juice**
Fresh, crisp vegetables, such as carrots, celery, and pepper strips

Combine all ingredients, except vegetables, in a medium bowl. Refrigerate for at least one hour, allowing flavors to blend. Makes 2 cups dip.

Serve with fresh vegetables such as carrots, celery, pepper strips, cauliflower, cucumbers, and zucchini. For crisp vegetables, prepare and place in Ziploc bags. Fill with small amount of water and refrigerate overnight. Drain and serve.

Teriyaki Buffalo Wings

"Wing it" with this easy recipe.

2½   **pounds frozen chicken wings**
1   **(10-ounce) bottle teriyaki sauce**

Take chicken wings from freezer and place in refrigerator to thaw overnight. The next morning, place wings in a Ziploc bag. Pour bottle of teriyaki sauce over the wings and refrigerate. Marinate all day, turning Ziploc bag occasionally. Place wings on a jelly-roll pan (15x10x1-inch). Pour teriyaki marinade left in bag over wings. Bake at 350 degrees for about 1 hour and 15 minutes. After the first 40 minutes, turn chicken to allow for even caramelizing.

Sweet-and-Sour Meatballs

These spirited meatballs are easy to make in the oven.

2   **pounds ground beef**
2   **teaspoons salt**
1   **small onion, finely chopped**
1   **cup soft bread crumbs**
½   **cup milk**
1   **recipe Sauce for Meatballs (see below)**

Combine all ingredients, except sauce, in a large bowl. Form into balls, using level tablespoon as measure. Place on a greased baking sheet and cook at 400 degrees for about 10 minutes or until cooked through. Makes about 72 meatballs.

SAUCE FOR MEATBALLS

2   **cups ketchup**
1   **cup grape jelly**

Mix ketchup and grape jelly in a small saucepan. Warm briefly over medium heat. Pour sauce over cooked meatballs. To serve, keep warm in small Crock-Pot or serving dish on warming tray. Can be made a day ahead and reheated.

Mud Pie Brownies

Wow!

- 4 eggs
- 2 cups sugar
- 1 cup butter or margarine, softened
- ⅓ cup unsweetened cocoa, or 2 squares melted unsweetened chocolate
- 1½ cups flour
- 1 tablespoon vanilla
- 2 cups chopped pecans or walnuts
- 1 cup flaked coconut
- 1 (7-ounce) jar Marshmallow Crème
- 1 recipe Chocolate Frosting (see next column)

In a large bowl, beat together eggs, sugar, and butter or margarine. Beat in cocoa or melted chocolate and flour. Stir in nuts and coconut. Pour batter into a greased 9x13-inch aluminum pan. Bake at 350 degrees for about 30 minutes. While brownies are baking, make Chocolate Frosting. Remove brownies from oven. While hot, spread with Marshmallow Crème, then swirl in Chocolate Frosting. Makes 15 brownies.

CHOCOLATE FROSTING

- ½ cup butter or margarine
- ¼ cup milk
- 3 tablespoons unsweetened cocoa
- 1 teaspoon vanilla
- 2 cups powdered sugar

In a large saucepan, melt butter over medium heat. Stir in milk, cocoa, and vanilla until well blended. Add powdered sugar and stir in. Use hand mixer to beat until smooth.

VALENTINE DINNER FOR TWO

Valentine's Day is filled with memories of hearts, cupids, pink, red, lace, and frills. You might remember decorating valentine boxes at school and wondering who would put a valentine inside and what it might say. You might still like candy hearts that say "Be Mine," "Cutie Pie," or "Hugs." Making your own valentines can still be a wonderful way to say "I care." And it's always fun to surprise someone by delivering homemade cookies or candies, or a dazzling dessert.

If you're looking for another way to show love and appreciation on Valentine's Day, try making a special meal. It could be a breakfast, lunch, or dinner. The following dinner is both elegant and easy and may be modified to feed two or twenty. Cornish Game Hens are spectacular on a dinner plate served with Barley and Pine Nuts. Baked salmon, halibut fillets, or sizzling steaks are also marvelous choices. Honey-Glazed Carrots complement any of these main dishes, and Strawberries and Fieldgreens Salad will add just the right touch to this romantic meal. Crème Brûlée served with Lace Cookies could be the perfect ending; unless, of course, you choose the equally fantastic Cream Puffs. Soft Sugar Cookies (see recipe on page 61) cut in heart shapes also make a nice ending or gift for your sweetheart.

Enjoy!

Cornish Game Hens

Dazzle the one you adore with this elegant dish.

2 (20-ounce) Cornish game hens
¼ teaspoon salt
¼ teaspoon pepper
¼ cup plum jam
Red leaf lettuce

Place hens in a small baking dish; sprinkle with salt and pepper and cover loosely with foil. Bake at 350 degrees for about 45 minutes. Remove foil. Baste with drippings. Bake uncovered for an additional 15 minutes or until tender and lightly browned. Remove from oven. Brush plum jam over surface of hens as glaze. Serve over Barley and Pine Nuts. Garnish the plate with red leaf lettuce. Makes 2 servings

Baked Salmon or Halibut Fillets

Seafood fans will love these.

½ cup plain yogurt
½ cup finely crushed Ritz® crackers
2 (½-pound) salmon or halibut fillets
1 lemon

Place yogurt on one plate and crushed crackers on another. Coat both sides of fillets with yogurt, then crushed crackers. Place fillets in well-greased baking dish. Bake at 450 degrees for about 10 to 15 minutes, or until cooked through. Serve with lemon wedges. Makes 2 generous servings.

Barley and Pine Nuts

You'll be nuts about this "hearty" dish.

½ cup chopped onion
¼ cup pine nuts or slivered almonds
¼ cup chopped fresh parsley (optional)
2 tablespoons butter
1 (14-ounce) can chicken broth
½ cup pearl barley

Sauté onion, nuts, and parsley in butter over medium heat until lightly browned (about 10 minutes). Place in small casserole dish. Stir in chicken broth and barley. Bake at 350 degrees, uncovered, for about 1 hour. Makes 2 large servings.

Honey-Glazed Carrots

Enjoy a touch of sweetness.

1½ cups sliced carrots
2 tablespoons butter
¼ cup chicken broth
¼ cup honey
¼ teaspoon salt
⅛ teaspoon pepper

Place carrots, butter, and broth in a medium saucepan and cook, covered, over medium heat for 5 minutes. Remove lid from pan. Stir in honey, salt, and pepper and cook another 15 minutes or until carrots are tender. Makes 2 servings.

Refrigerator Biscuits

Have a heart!

1 (.25-ounce) package dry yeast

½ cup warm water

5 cups flour

3 tablespoons sugar

1 tablespoon baking powder

1 teaspoon baking soda

1 teaspoon salt

1 cup butter or shortening

2 cups buttermilk

Dissolve yeast in ½ cup warm water. Let stand 10 minutes. In a large bowl, sift together flour, sugar, baking powder, baking soda, and salt. Cut in the shortening or butter with a pastry cutter or two knives. In a separate bowl, combine buttermilk and dissolved yeast mixture; add to dry mixture, stirring only until moistened. Put dough in a large plastic container. Cover and refrigerate for several hours before baking. Dough can be stored in refrigerator for up to one week.

When ready to bake, carefully roll out dough to ½-inch thickness on a well-floured surface. Cut desired number of biscuits with a heart-shaped cookie cutter. (Refrigerate remaining dough to use with meals during the week.) Place biscuits on a greased baking sheet. Bake at 400 degrees for about 15 minutes or until golden. Makes 3 dozen biscuits.

Strawberries and Fieldgreens Salad

It will be "love at first sight."

1 cup greens of your choice, such as red or green leaf lettuce or spinach

1 cup sliced strawberries, lightly sprinkled with sugar

1 recipe Sesame Vinaigrette Dressing (see below)

Place ½ cup greens on each plate. Top with ½ cup strawberries. Spoon desired amount of Sesame Vinaigrette Dressing over each salad. Serves 2.

SESAME VINAIGRETTE DRESSING

¼ cup red wine vinegar

⅓ cup sugar

2 teaspoons minced onion

¼ teaspoon Worcestershire sauce

¼ teaspoon paprika

½ cup olive or vegetable oil

2 tablespoons sesame seeds

Place all ingredients except sesame seeds in blender and mix well. Stir in sesame seeds. Keeps in the refrigerator up to 2 weeks.

VALENTINE DINNER FOR TWO

Crème Brûlée

This is an elegant, easy dessert.

> 3   **eggs**
> ¼   **cup packed brown sugar**
> ½   **teaspoon vanilla**
> 1½   **cups cream or half-and-half**
> 2   **tablespoons brown sugar, for the caramelized tops**

Place a shallow baking pan on the middle rack of the oven. In a medium bowl, lightly whisk eggs with the ¼ cup brown sugar and vanilla. Gradually stir in cream or half-and-half; pour into 2 custard cups or ramekins. Place ramekins on baking pan and pour enough water into pan to come halfway up the ramekins. Bake at 325 degrees for about 45 minutes or until set around the edges but still soft in the center. Remove cups from pan. Chill for at least 2 hours or up to 2 days.

When ready to serve, press about 2 tablespoons of brown sugar through a strainer and sprinkle over tops of crème brûlée. Place ramekins under broiler on middle-top rack until sugar melts; watch carefully to prevent scorching. Chill for at least a few minutes before serving for sugar to become crisp. Serve within two hours of broiling. Makes 2 servings.

Lace Cookies

These romantic, delicate cookies are surprisingly simple.

> ¼   **cup flour**
> ⅛   **teaspoon baking powder**
> ¼   **cup sugar**
> ¼   **cup quick Quaker® oats**
> ¼   **cup pecans, finely chopped**
> 1   **tablespoon cream**
> 3   **tablespoons butter, melted**
> 1   **tablespoon corn syrup**
> ½   **cup chocolate chips (optional)**

Line one large baking sheet with parchment paper. In a small mixing bowl, stir together flour, baking powder, sugar, quick Quaker® Oats, and pecans. Stir in cream, melted butter, and corn syrup until well blended. Drop mixture by level tablespoons onto parchment-lined baking sheet several inches apart. Bake only 3 cookies at a time. Bake at 325 degrees for about 10 to 15 minutes or until lightly browned. Remove cookie sheet from oven. Allow cookies to cool for about 2 minutes. While still hot, but able to handle, use a spatula to remove cookies and drape over a rolling pin (top side down) to completely cool. Slide cookies off rolling pin and place on a plate. Repeat the above steps to make remaining cookies. If desired, melt chocolate chips in the microwave at 20-second intervals just until melted. Spoon chocolate over half of one side of each cooled cookie. Place on parchment paper and allow to dry. Cookies can be made a day in advance and stored in an airtight container. Makes 6 cookies.

Cream Puffs

You'll love these!

- 1   **cup water**
- ½   **cup butter**
- 1   **cup flour**
- 4   **eggs**
- 1   **recipe Cream Puff Filling (see next column)**

Bring water and butter to boil in a large saucepan; remove pan from heat. Immediately add flour all at once and stir vigorously with wooden spoon until mixture leaves pan and forms a ball (about 1 to 2 minutes). Add eggs, one at a time, beating vigorously after each addition until smooth. Drop by heaping tablespoonfuls onto a 15½x10½x1-inch greased baking sheet, allowing room for expansion. Bake at 400 degrees for about 25 to 30 minutes or until puffed and golden. Remove and cool while preparing filling.

To fill, cut puffs horizontally with sharp knife, removing lid. Scoop out any soft dough. Fill shells generously with Cream Puff Filling. Replace lids. Shells and filling can be made a day in advance and refrigerated. Fill the shells the day of serving. Makes 12 large or 20 small cream puffs. If you choose this dessert with the Valentine Dinner for Two, you can give the remaining cream puffs to someone as a Valentine's Day gift.

CREAM PUFF FILLING

- 1   **(6-ounce) package vanilla instant pudding**
- 2   **cups milk**
- 1   **cup whipping cream**

Prepare pudding as directed on package, using only 2 cups milk. Refrigerate for at least 30 minutes. Whip cream. Gently blend pudding with whipped cream. Makes enough filling for 1 recipe Cream Puffs.

PRESIDENTS' DAY PICNIC

Picnics aren't just for summer; and Presidents' Day may be the perfect time to pack a simple meal and head outdoors for an adventure. Some of life's memorable moments may be awaiting you. Make the most of a snowy winter day by soaring downhill on a sled, snowboarding, skiing, snowshoeing, skating, building a snowman, or just enjoying nature. Perhaps you'll see a deer or rabbit on the run as the slopes sparkle in the sun.

Pausing for a picnic will brighten your day. Make it simple. Choose a "hot" picnic that suits your fancy and enjoy. For quick snacking and refreshment, pack fruit slices, such as oranges, bananas, and apples (sprinkled with lemon juice so they stay fresh). Or, consider crisp carrot and celery sticks. To crisp vegetables, slice and dice as desired then place in Ziploc bags. Fill bags with a small amount of water and refrigerate overnight. Drain before serving.

Remember to pack a plastic tarp to insure a dry place to sit; gather other outdoor supplies and any equipment that may be needed.

If there's no snow in sight, plan another adventure—perhaps at the beach or lake. Or, you may decide to go walking, hiking, biking, or exploring a new horizon. You may want to choose a menu from another section in the book. As the sun begins to sink in the sky, feel the joy of being in the great outdoors with family or friends on a winter day.

MENU ONE

Minestrone Soup

Warm up with this savory soup!

1   **pound pork sausage**

4   **cups water**

2   **stalks celery, diced**

2   **large carrots, diced**

1   **medium onion, diced**

1   **(10-ounce) can beef broth**

1   **(10-ounce) can bean with bacon soup**

1   **(28-ounce) can diced tomatoes**

1   **tablespoon sugar**

2   **cloves garlic, minced, or 1 teaspoon garlic salt**

1   **teaspoon dried oregano**

1   **teaspoon salt**

½   **teaspoon pepper**

Brown sausage in a large pot. Add remaining ingredients and stir together. Simmer, uncovered, over low heat for at least 1 hour. This soup is best if made a day in advance. On the picnic day, heat soup and place in a thermos to keep hot for the picnic. Makes about 10 cups.

Parmesan Breadsticks

Perfect for pack-and-go.

1   **loaf Rhodes® frozen bread dough**

¼   **cup butter, melted**

½   **cup grated Parmesan cheese**

Thaw bread dough for about 2 hours. Cut loaf into eight pieces; stretch each piece to about 6 inches. Dip in butter and then roll in Parmesan cheese. Place on greased baking sheet. Let rise 30 minutes. Bake at 400 degrees for about 12 minutes or until lightly browned. Makes 8 large breadsticks.

Soft Gingersnap Cookies

Spice up the celebration with these delicious cookies.

- ¾ **cup butter or margarine, softened**
- 1 **cup packed brown sugar**
- 1 **egg**
- ¼ **cup molasses**
- 2¼ **cups flour**
- 2 **teaspoons baking soda**
- 1 **teaspoon cinnamon**
- 1 **teaspoon ginger**
- ½ **teaspoon ground cloves**
- ¼ **teaspoon salt**
  Granulated sugar

Cream together butter or margarine, brown sugar, egg, and molasses. In a separate bowl, combine all remaining ingredients except granulated sugar; add to creamed mixture and beat together. Cover bowl and chill in refrigerator for at least 1 hour. Using 1 tablespoon as a measure, roll dough into balls, making about 24 dough balls. Dip tops in granulated sugar. Place balls, sugared side up, on greased baking sheets about 3 inches apart. Bake at 350 degrees for 10 to 12 minutes. Immediately remove cookies from baking sheets and cool on wire racks. Makes 24 large cookies.

MENU TWO

Beef Buns

The beef stays warm in a thermos.

- 1 **6- or 7-pound beef chuck roast**
- 2 **tablespoons olive oil or butter**
- 1 **(1-ounce) package dry onion soup mix**
- 1 **cup water**
- 1 **(10.5-ounce) can beef consommé**
- 12 **large buns**

Heat olive oil or butter in a large roasting pan or other oven-proof pot. Brown roast well on all sides; sprinkle with onion soup mix. Pour water and consommé over roast. Cover with lid. Bake at 325 degrees for about 4 hours or until meat is tender. Remove from oven. When cooled, place meat on surface for cutting, reserving drippings in pan. Slice meat and return to pan. Reheat and simmer, uncovered, for about 30 minutes. Place warm beef and drippings in a thermos. Fill buns at serving time. Serves 12, with extra for second servings.

Broccoli-Bacon Pasta Salad

This salad travels well.

- 4 spears fresh broccoli, chopped
- 2 pounds bacon, fried crisp, drained, and crumbled
- 1 red onion, chopped
- 1 pound fresh mushrooms, sliced
- 2 pounds pasta of your choice, cooked and drained
- 1 cup roasted sunflower seeds (optional)
- 1 recipe Pasta Dressing (see below)

Place all ingredients in a large bowl. Pour Pasta Dressing over top and gently stir. Chill for several hours. Makes 12 servings.

PASTA DRESSING

- 2 cups mayonnaise
- ½ cup red wine vinegar
- 1 cup sugar

Combine ingredients. Stir well.

Wassail

The spicy fragrance fills the air.

- 8 cups apple juice or cider
- 2 cups orange juice
- 1 cup fresh lemon juice
- 1 cup sugar
- ½ teaspoon ground cloves
- ½ teaspoon allspice
- ½ teaspoon cinnamon

Combine all ingredients in a large pot; bring to a boil. Reduce heat and simmer uncovered for 15 minutes. Keep hot in a thermos. Makes about 12 cups.

Cherry Dump Cake

Throw this dessert together in a hurry.

- 2 (21-ounce) cans cherry pie filling
- ½ teaspoon almond extract (optional)
- 1 package yellow cake mix
- ½ cup butter or margarine, melted
  Whipped cream, for topping
  Ice cream, if desired

Combine cherry pie filling and almond extract, then pour into a 9x13-inch baking dish. Sprinkle cake mix over cherries. Melt butter and pour evenly over cake mix. Bake at 350 degrees for 35 to 40 minutes. Serve warm with whipped cream or ice cream. May also be made with a chocolate cake mix. Makes about 12 servings.

SPRING

ST. PATRICK'S DAY DINNER

As legend tells us, wearing green on St. Patrick's Day brings good luck. So, how about a menu dressed in green and loaded with tradition to make you and yours even luckier? You certainly don't need to be Irish to enjoy food, music, and fun.

There are many naturally green fresh foods to make your table festive: artichokes, lettuce, spinach, pistachios, broccoli, kiwifruit, avocados, peas, and beans to name but a few. Pick and choose as you wish; use your imagination and creativity. Corned Beef and Cabbage in the Crock-Pot is a time-honored favorite. Sweet and Sour Cabbage Rolls are zesty and delicious. Top off the meal with luscious Pistachio Pudding Squares or Shamrock Chocolate Cookies—they'll disappear like magic. Gather together around the table, throw in some Irish laughter, and celebrate. Don't be surprised if someone does an Irish jig.

Corned Beef and Cabbage in the Crock-Pot

It's your lucky day!

- 2   pounds small red potatoes
- 2   cups baby carrots
- 1   onion, cut in large wedges
- 1   3-pound corned beef brisket with seasoning packet
      Water
- ½   head of cabbage, cut in wedges
- ¼   cup butter, melted
      Salt and pepper to taste

Place potatoes, carrots, and onions in a 5- to 6½-quart Crock-Pot. Top with corned beef brisket; sprinkle with seasoning packet. Add enough water just to cover brisket. Cover with lid. Cook on high setting for about 8 hours or until meat is tender. Add cabbage wedges to Crock-Pot and continue cooking for about 15 minutes or until cabbage is tender. To serve, remove corned beef from Crock-Pot; place on a platter and cut beef across grain into thin slices. Remove vegetables from Crock-Pot with a slotted spoon; place around the beef. Pour butter over vegetables, and salt and pepper to taste. Makes 6 servings.

Irish Soda Bread

Enjoy on St. Patrick's Day or any other time.

- 2   cups flour
- 2   tablespoons sugar
- 1   teaspoon baking soda
- 2   teaspoons baking powder
- ½   teaspoon salt
- 3   tablespoons butter
- ½   cup raisins (optional)
- 1   cup buttermilk
- 1   tablespoon butter, melted
      Flour to dust

In a large bowl, sift together flour, sugar, baking soda, baking powder, and salt. Cut in butter until mixture looks like fine crumbs. Add raisins, if desired. Add buttermilk. Mix with a fork until moistened.

Knead gently about 1 minute. Shape into a ball. Place dough on a greased cookie sheet or pie plate and flatten into a 7-inch circle. Dough will be about 1½ inches thick. Bake at 375 degrees for 30 to 40 minutes, or until top is golden brown. Remove and place on a wire rack to cool. Brush top with melted butter. Dust with flour. Makes 1 loaf.

Sweet-and-Sour Cabbage Rolls

An old favorite.

- 2 pounds ground beef
- 1 cup cooked rice
- ½ teaspoon ground thyme
- 1 teaspoon salt
- ½ teaspoon pepper
- ¼ teaspoon garlic salt
- 1 (8-ounce) can tomato sauce
- ¾ cup finely diced onion
- 2 cloves garlic, minced
- 1 large head green cabbage
- 1 recipe Sweet-and-Sour Sauce (see next column)

Combine all ingredients except cabbage and Sweet-and-Sour Sauce; mix well and set aside. Microwave rinsed whole cabbage for 4 minutes on high power. Carefully remove whole individual cabbage leaves from head. Fill one leaf at a time with meat mixture, about ½ cup—or enough to fill adequately. Do not overstuff. Fold burrito style, making about 10 cabbage rolls. Place rolls in a 9x13-inch dish. Pour Sweet-and-Sour Sauce over cabbage rolls; cover dish loosely with foil. Bake at 350 degrees for about 40 minutes or until beef is done. Makes about 10 cabbage rolls. Tastes great when served with rice and Carrots and Onions.

SWEET-AND-SOUR SAUCE

- 2 (16-ounce) cans tomato sauce
- ¼ teaspoon garlic salt
- ¼ teaspoon pepper
- ½ cup lemon juice or vinegar
- 1 cup brown sugar

Combine all ingredients in a medium bowl. Use as directed for Sweet-and-Sour Cabbage Rolls.

Carrots and Onions

These go well with many meals.

- 2 cups water
- 4 cups baby carrots
- 1 onion, cut in large wedges
  Butter, to taste
  Salt and pepper, to taste

In a saucepan, bring 2 cups of water to a boil. Add carrots and onion wedges; return to a boil. Reduce heat to medium-low and simmer until vegetables are tender. Pour off water. Toss with butter, salt, and pepper to taste. Makes 6 servings.

Pistachio Pudding Squares

Eyes will be smiling after eating these squares.

½   **cup butter or margarine**

⅓   **cup sugar**

2   **teaspoons water**

1   **cup flour**

1   **teaspoon vanilla**

½   **cup pecans, walnuts, or cashews, chopped**

1   **(6-ounce) package vanilla instant pudding**

3   **(3.4-ounce) packages pistachio instant pudding**

6   **cups milk, divided**

2   **cups whipping cream, plus sugar to sweeten**

For the crust, cream butter and sugar together in a large bowl. Add water, flour, vanilla, and nuts; mix well. Spread mixture in a greased 9x13-inch pan. Bake at 350 degrees for 10 to 12 minutes, until light brown. Set aside to cool.

Prepare vanilla pudding according to package directions, using 2 cups of milk; spread over cooled crust. Chill to set. Prepare pistachio pudding according to package directions, using the remaining 4 cups milk; spread over vanilla pudding to make second layer. Chill to set. Before serving, whip and sweeten cream. Top with sweetened whipped cream. Serves 12 to 15.

Shamrock Chocolate Cookies

These cookies will bring you the luck o' the Irish.

½   **cup butter or margarine, softened**

¾   **cup sugar**

1   **egg**

1   **teaspoon vanilla**

1½   **cups flour**

⅓   **cup unsweetened cocoa**

½   **teaspoon baking powder**

½   **teaspoon baking soda**

¼   **teaspoon salt**

1   **recipe Shamrock Glaze (see below)**

In a large bowl, cream butter, sugar, egg, and vanilla until light and fluffy. In a separate bowl, combine flour, cocoa, baking powder, baking soda, and salt; add to creamed mixture, blending well. Chill about 1 hour or until firm enough to roll.

Roll out a small portion of dough at a time on a lightly floured board or between 2 pieces of waxed paper to ¼-inch thickness. Cut with shamrock shaped cookie cutter. Place on greased cookie sheet. Bake at 325 degrees for 5 to 7 minutes. Cool and glaze. Makes about 2 dozen cookies.

SHAMROCK GLAZE

3   **tablespoons butter or margarine**

2   **cups powdered sugar**

1   **teaspoon vanilla**

2 to 3   **tablespoons milk**
         Green food coloring

In a small saucepan, melt butter over low heat; remove from heat and blend in sugar and vanilla. Gradually add milk; beat well. Blend in 2 or 3 drops green food coloring.

EASTER DINNER

Easter is a glorious time of joy and rebirth: delicate buds begin to blossom; purple crocuses and pink hyacinths line stone paths; and children gather a rainbow of pastel eggs in baskets. Bouquets of nodding tulips, violets, and primroses brighten dinner tables as families gather together for foods as fresh as spring.

The following menu will fill your home with spicy fragrances as everyone waits for the grand centerpiece to make its entrance: Baked Ham with Sauce or Roast Leg of Lamb, depending on your family's taste. Side dishes made from new potatoes, garden peas, whole carrots, and strawberries will bring color and freshness to the table. Sunshine Dessert, a creamy lemon delight, will be an elegant ending to a perfect Easter meal, which could be served for brunch or lunch as well.

After dinner, enjoy a spring walk together. Perhaps you'll come upon a buttercup bank with a brooklet running by or a meadow filled with forget-me-nots. Maybe someone will spot a bird's nest high in a blossoming tree. You're sure to feel gratitude for the promise of spring and the Savior's priceless gift of life.

Jerusalem Artichoke and Spinach Dip

Serve with crackers or baguette bread slices.

2 (10-ounce) boxes frozen chopped spinach

½ cup chopped onion

¼ cup butter, melted

1 (8-ounce) package cream cheese, softened

2 (8-ounce) jars artichoke hearts, drained and chopped

8 ounces Monterey Jack cheese, grated

1 teaspoon garlic salt

¼ cup grated Parmesan cheese
   Baguette bread slices and crackers

Cook spinach according to package directions; drain well and squeeze out liquid. Microwave onions in butter for 2 minutes on high power. Combine cooked spinach, onion mixture, cream cheese, artichoke hearts, Monterey Jack cheese, and garlic salt in a medium bowl; mix well. Place in a greased baking dish. Bake at 350 degrees for 30 minutes. Remove from oven and sprinkle with Parmesan cheese. Return to oven for about 10 minutes or until cheese melts. Serve with baguette bread slices and crackers. Makes about 2 cups dip.

Baked Ham with Sauce

The sweet, spicy aroma of this ham is irresistible.

1 (4-pound) precooked, sliced ham

½ cup packed brown sugar

½ cup apricot jam

¼ cup Worcestershire sauce

Place ham in a roasting pan. In a small saucepan, combine brown sugar, apricot jam, and Worcestershire sauce. Warm through, stirring until sugar is dissolved. Spoon half of the sauce over surface of ham. Reserve remaining sauce for individual servings. Bake at 325 degrees for about 30 minutes, just until warmed through. Overcooking will result in dryness. Makes 12 servings.

Roast Leg of Lamb

This is a traditional favorite.

- 1 **leg of lamb (about 6 pounds)**
  Salt and pepper, to taste
- 3 **cloves garlic, peeled and slivered**
  Fresh rosemary sprigs

Rub lamb with salt and pepper. With point of sharp knife, cut small slits in skin; stuff with garlic slivers and rosemary. Place in a roasting pan and roast at 350 degrees for about 1¼ hours. Internal temperature should read 130 degrees for rare meat or 145 degrees for medium doneness on an instant-read meat thermometer. If you prefer your lamb well done, roast 10 minutes more. Remove from oven and let stand about 15 minutes before carving. Makes about 12 servings.

Creamed Peas and New Potatoes

Enjoy the tastes of spring.

- 4 **pounds baby red potatoes**
- 1 **cup butter**
- 1 **cup flour**
- 8 **cups milk or half-and-half**
- 1 **tablespoon salt**
- 2 **(10-ounce) packages frozen peas**

Place potatoes in a large cooking pot. Fill with water just to cover potatoes. Cook for about 30 minutes over medium heat or until potatoes are tender. Pour off water and set aside. In a saucepan, melt butter over medium heat. Add flour and stir until well blended. Gradually stir in milk or half-and-half. Stir constantly until mixture comes to a full boil. Continue cooking 2 to 3 minutes or until thickened. Remove from heat; stir in salt. Add potatoes. About 5 minutes before serving, stir in frozen peas. Warm and stir until thoroughly heated through. Makes 12 servings.

Whole Carrots

Try serving carrots this fun way.

- 12 **whole carrots (medium size with green tops)**
- 4 **cups water**
  Butter, to taste
  Salt and pepper, to taste
  Fresh parsley, chopped

Peel carrots, leaving green tops intact. In a large pot, cook carrots in water for about 10 minutes or until tender; drain. Salt, pepper, and butter to taste. Sprinkle lightly with fresh parsley. Makes 12 servings.

Feather-Light Overnight Rolls

These rolls are light and irresistible. You can freeze shaped dough for later use.

1 **cup water**

1 **cup butter**

¾ **cup sugar**

2 **teaspoons salt**

1 **cup cold water**

2 **(.25-ounce) packages yeast**

½ **cup warm water**

4 **beaten eggs**

7½ **cups flour**

Butter for spreading on dough

In a 6-quart pan bring the 1 cup water to a boil. Add the 1 cup butter, sugar, and salt; remove from heat. Add the 1 cup cold water. Dissolve yeast in ½ cup warm water (not hot). When first mixture is lukewarm, add yeast mixture and beaten eggs. Stir briefly. Add flour and stir together. Cover pan with lid and refrigerate overnight. When ready to roll out, divide dough in thirds. Lightly flour the surface of a bread board. Roll out each third in a large circle about ½-inch thick. Spread dough lightly with butter. Cut dough into 12 wedges and roll each up, beginning at the wide end, to form a crescent shape. Place on 3 greased baking sheets (12 rolls per sheet). Let rise for 4 hours. Bake at 400 degrees for about 12 minutes or until lightly browned. Makes 3 dozen rolls.

Note: If making ahead, freeze after dough has been shaped into crescent rolls and placed on baking sheets. Once frozen, rolls can be placed in plastic freezer bags. When ready to use, return rolls to cookie sheets and let rise about 6 hours or until light. Proceed with baking instructions.

Fresh Strawberries

Simply delicious!

2 **quarts (8 cups) strawberries**

½ **cup sugar**

About an hour before serving time, wash strawberries; remove stems; and cut into thick slices. Sprinkle with sugar and gently stir. Makes about 12 servings.

Sunshine Dessert

This overnight sensation is spectacular!

	Half of a large round angel food cake
2½	cups milk
1	cup whipping cream
1	(3.5-ounce) package sour cream instant pudding
1	(3.5-ounce) package lemon instant pudding
¾	cup slivered almonds, toasted
1	recipe Orange-Mandarin Sauce (see next column)
	Raspberries or strawberries and kiwifruit, for garnishing

In a greased 9x13-inch pan, break half of an angel food cake into golf-ball-size pieces. Set aside. Reserve other cake half for another use or for a second Sunshine Dessert. In a bowl, combine milk and whipping cream. Beat in the pudding mixes and continue beating until well mixed. When mix begins to thicken, pour evenly over the cake pieces. Sprinkle nuts over the top. Chill overnight. At serving time, cut into squares and place on individual dishes. Top with Orange-Mandarin Sauce. Garnish with either a raspberry or a strawberry half and a slice of kiwifruit cut in half. Makes 12 servings.

ORANGE-MANDARIN SAUCE

1	(15-ounce) can mandarin oranges
1	cup sugar
¼	cup cornstarch
2	cups orange juice
3	tablespoons fresh lemon juice

Drain mandarin oranges well; set aside. In a saucepan, combine sugar and cornstarch; add orange juice and bring to a boil, stirring constantly. Cook and stir for 1 to 2 minutes or until thickened. Remove from heat. Stir in lemon juice. Add mandarin oranges. Chill overnight.

Little Nests

These are adorable as place cards or favors, and they taste good too! Children will like helping in their preparation.

- ¼ **cup butter or margarine**
- 1 **cup miniature marshmallows**
- 1 **cup All-Bran® or Fiber One® cereal**
- 1 **small package mini robin eggs (Whoppers®)**

In a small saucepan, melt butter or margarine over low heat. Add miniature marshmallows. Stir until marshmallows are melted. Remove from heat; add cereal and stir just until coated. When cool enough to handle, form into eight little nests. Place on waxed paper. After about 1 hour, press in center of each nest to form indention. Place three robin eggs in center of each nest. Place on a 3- or 4-inch doily and use as place cards or favors. Makes 8 nests.

APRIL SHOWERS

April showers bring May flowers. They also help celebrate weddings or baby arrivals. The plans for your shower can vary from simple to elaborate. You might prefer casual occasions, with conversation and gift-opening as the focus. You could also choose to include games, photos, predictions, bows in the hair, memories, and advice from family and friends. There are many food choices as well, depending on the number of guests and hostesses involved. The following two menu ideas will get you thinking.

The first menu features Haystacks, which guests can create by stacking their own plates with rice, a chicken mixture, and condiments. A salad bar—including items such as tomatoes, crumbled bacon, asparagus, bleu cheese, sunflower seeds, cheese, and so on—is also a nice build-your-own-meal idea. Simply delicious Orange Rolls complement either choice. Butterscotch Brownies are wonderful and Raspberry-Pineapple Sherbet refreshing. Hostesses can divide up the responsibilities. If you want to simplify the menu, the Haystacks and Orange Rolls could be the meal, excluding the brownies and sherbet. The brownies and sherbet could also stand alone as dessert refreshments for a shower.

The second menu gives you a choice of Ham-and-Cheese Croissants or Chicken Salad Croissants, Raspberry-Lemonade Slush, Fresh Fruit, and Chocolate Mint Brownies. If you want to serve in a novel way, this menu works well for a box lunch. Putting together the boxes in advance takes some time and planning; but if you get an assembly line going, you'll all have fun. When everything is all boxed up, watch for smiles as each guest picks up her own box and unties the colorful ribbon. The hostesses will be free to join in the fun of the party—giving a warm send-off to a bride and groom or rejoicing in the arrival of a new family member.

These menus are also wonderful for meals following special occasions, such as homecomings, baby blessings, or baptisms.

MENU ONE

Haystacks

Build your own.

2   **tablespoons butter**
½   **cup chopped onion**
1   **(26-ounce) can cream of chicken soup**
6   **cups cooked and diced chicken**
2   **cups sour cream**
8   **cups cooked rice**
1   **(9.5-ounce) can chow mein noodles**
2   **(20-ounce) cans pineapple tidbits, drained**
2   **(15-ounce) cans mandarin oranges, drained**
1   **cup sliced green onions**
1   **cup chopped celery**
1   **cup chopped red pepper**
2   **cups frozen green peas, thawed**
1   **cup flaked coconut**
½   **cup slivered almonds, toasted**

In a saucepan, sauté butter and onions for about 3 minutes. Add chicken soup and warm over medium heat. Stir in chicken and sour cream and cook until hot, but do not boil. Place on the serving table in a Crock-Pot or chafing dish to keep warm. Place rice and toppings in separate bowls on a buffet table. Guests build their own haystacks by placing a bed of rice on a plate, then spooning on chicken mixture and toppings as desired. Makes about 12 servings.

Orange Rolls

Preparing for a crowd will be easy.

½   **cup butter, melted**
½   **cup sugar**
1   **orange peel, grated**
18   **Rhodes® frozen dinner rolls**
1   **recipe Orange Glaze (see below)**

Combine melted butter, sugar, and grated orange peel in a bowl. Dip rolls in mixture and place in greased muffin tins. Allow to rise for four hours. Bake at 350 degrees for 10 to 15 minutes or until lightly browned. Frost with Orange Glaze while still warm. Makes 18 rolls.

ORANGE GLAZE

1   **cup powdered sugar**
2   **tablespoons butter, softened**
2   **tablespoons orange juice**

Mix ingredients together.

Butterscotch Brownies

They'll be in love with these.

¾	cup butter or margarine
3	cups packed brown sugar
3	eggs, beaten
2¼	cups flour
2	teaspoons baking powder
¾	teaspoon salt
1	teaspoon vanilla
1	cup pecans or walnuts, chopped
1	cup flaked coconut

In a large saucepan, melt butter or margarine over low heat; remove from heat and cool. Blend in brown sugar and eggs. In a separate bowl, mix together flour, baking powder, and salt; add to first mixture and blend well. Stir in vanilla, nuts, and coconut. Spread in greased 9x13-inch pan and bake at 350 degrees for about 30 to 35 minutes. Makes about 15 bars.

Raspberry-Pineapple Sherbet

Refreshing!

½	gallon pineapple sherbet
2	(10-ounce) packages frozen raspberries, undrained
4	bananas, sliced
	Ginger ale or lemon-lime soda (optional)

Let sherbet and raspberries soften slightly. Place sherbet in a plastic container and stir well. Stir in bananas. Gently add raspberries. Cover and freeze. Serve as a sherbet or as a slush by adding ginger ale or soda to desired consistency. Makes about 12 servings.

Ham-and-Cheese Croissants

Yum! Warm and wonderful!

- 20 **small croissants**
- 2 **pounds (20 slices) precooked ham**
- 1 **(8-ounce) package presliced Monterey Jack cheese (10 slices)**

Cut croissants three-quarters of the way through. (Cutting from the back side of the croissant makes for easy cutting and filling.) Fill each croissant with 1 slice of ham. Cut cheese slices in half. Place one piece on top of each slice of ham. Place filled croissants on large baking sheet. Cover with foil. Bake at 300 degrees for about 10 minutes or just until cheese is melted. Serve immediately. Makes 20 croissants.

Chicken Salad Croissants

Everyone's favorite.

- 4 **cups cooked and cubed chicken breasts**
- 1 **cup chopped celery or water chestnuts**
- 2 **teaspoons grated onion or finely chopped green onion**
- 1 **(20-ounce) can pineapple tidbits, drained**
- ½ **cup seedless red or green grapes, cut in half**
- ⅔ **cup mayonnaise**
- 1 **teaspoon salt**
- ⅛ **teaspoon pepper**
- 20 **small croissants**

Combine chicken, celery, onion, pineapple, and grapes in a large bowl. In a separate bowl, mix together mayonnaise, salt, and pepper. Fold dressing into chicken mixture until well coated. Makes 8 cups filling. Fills 20 small croissants.

Raspberry-Lemonade Slush

Refreshing! Plan for refills.

- 6 **cups hot water**
- 4 **cups sugar**
- 1 **(12-ounce) can frozen lemonade concentrate**
- 1 **(16-ounce) can crushed pineapple with juice**
- 2 **(10-ounce) packages frozen raspberries**
- 2 **liters ginger ale or lemon-lime soda**

In a 5-quart ice cream bucket or similar container, combine hot water and sugar; stir until sugar is dissolved. Add lemonade, pineapple, and raspberries and stir until well mixed. Freeze overnight. Serve with desired amount of ginger ale or soda. Makes 10 to 12 servings.

Chocolate Mint Brownies

Layered, luscious chocolate melts in your mouth.

1   cup sugar

1   cup packed brown sugar

1   cup butter, softened

4   eggs

4   (1-ounce) squares baking chocolate

2   teaspoons vanilla

2   cups flour

¼   teaspoon baking powder

1   recipe Mint Frosting (see next column)

1   recipe Chocolate Glaze (see next column)

In a large bowl, cream together sugars and butter until fluffy. Beat in eggs until well blended; set aside. In a small bowl, microwave baking chocolate for 1 minute. Stir and continue to heat at 10-second intervals just until melted. Add melted chocolate to the sugar and butter mixture. Add vanilla. In a separate bowl, stir together flour and baking powder; add to creamed mixture and mix well. Spread batter into a greased 9x13-inch baking dish and bake at 325 degrees for about 25 minutes, or until a toothpick inserted in center comes out with a few fudgy crumbs. When brownies are cool, frost with Mint Frosting and refrigerate for an hour. Drizzle Chocolate Glaze over frosting before serving. Makes about 15 brownies.

MINT FROSTING

½   cup butter, softened

¼   cup milk

1   teaspoon peppermint extract

5   drops red or green food coloring

4   cups powdered sugar

Mix butter, milk, peppermint extract, and food coloring together. Add powdered sugar and mix well.

CHOCOLATE GLAZE

3   tablespoons butter

½   cup chocolate chips

1   teaspoon vanilla extract

Microwave butter and chocolate chips together on high power for one minute. Add vanilla and stir. Randomly drizzle glaze over frosted brownies.

Fresh Fruit

Celebrate the season.

1   head green leaf lettuce

4   cantaloupes

2   pounds strawberries

2   pounds red grapes, cut in 20 clusters

Wash and drain lettuce leaves well. Place one leaf on each plate. Cut each cantaloupe into 6 wedges. Remove rind. Place one wedge of cantaloupe, two strawberries, and a cluster of grapes on each leaf. Makes 20 servings.

CINCO DE MAYO

Mexican dancers in brightly colored swirling skirts, energetic trumpeters, mariachi bands, piñatas, and tasty spices; these are the images of Cinco de Mayo. Held every May 5, Cinco de Mayo celebrates the victory of Mexican patriots in battle in 1862. Wanting to capture and experience the energy and excitement associated with the holiday, many families with no clear-cut tie to Mexico have now added Cinco de Mayo to their list of occasions to celebrate. The best word to describe both the holiday and flavorful foods is *festive*.

Preparation for the event may be as much fun as the event itself. Children, grandchildren, and neighbors can help with stuffing tortillas, stacking tostadas, or making piñatas. Add fresh salsa, a squeeze of lime, and colorful fresh-fruit drinks to the mix, then revel in the excitement of Cinco de Mayo.

Green-Chile-and-Cheese Canapés

Olé! Let the celebration begin!

- 1 **cup low-fat Best Foods® mayonnaise**
- 1 **cup grated Monterey Jack cheese**
- 1 **(4-ounce) can chopped green chiles**
- 1 **clove garlic, minced**
- 1 **long loaf baguette French bread, thinly sliced**

In a bowl, combine mayonnaise and cheese; set aside. In another bowl, combine chiles and garlic. Spread chile-garlic mixture on each bread slice. Top with a tablespoon of mayonnaise and cheese mixture. Place on a baking sheet. Broil for about 3 minutes or until bubbly and slightly brown. Makes about 2 dozen.

   Note: This recipe calls for low-fat mayonnaise. Using both low-fat mayonnaise and low-fat sour cream in many of the recipes in this book will significantly cut the amount of fat used without compromising taste.

Taco Ranch Dip

The lime adds zip!

- 1½ **cups mayonnaise**
- ¾ **cup sour cream**
- ½ **cup buttermilk**
- 1 **(1.25-ounce) package taco seasoning**
- 2 **tablespoons fresh lime juice**

In a bowl, whisk ingredients together until well blended. Serve with assorted fresh vegetables or tortilla chips.

Chicken Taco Soup

So good!

- 6 **cups water**
- 6 **chicken bouillon cubes**
- 4 **chicken breasts, cooked and cubed**
- 1 **teaspoon cumin**
- 1 or 2 **tablespoons chili powder**
- 1 **(29-ounce) can crushed tomatoes**
- 1 **tablespoon sugar**
- ½ **cup rice**
- 1 **(15-ounce) can garbanzo beans, undrained**
  Corn chips
  Cheese, grated
  Cilantro, chopped
  Sour cream
- 2 **limes, quartered**

In a large pot, bring water to a boil; dissolve bouillon cubes. Reduce heat to low. Stir in cubed chicken, cumin, chili powder, tomatoes, sugar, rice, and garbanzo beans. Simmer for about 1 hour. When ready to serve, add remaining ingredients as toppings to individual servings. Makes about 8 servings.

Chicken Tostadas

El grande!

- 2 **tablespoons vegetable oil, plus more for cooking tortillas**
- 2 **pounds chicken tenders**
- 1 **clove garlic, minced**
- 1 **(4-ounce) can diced green chiles, drained**
- ½ **cup sour cream**
- 6 **(6-inch) flour tortillas**
- ½ **small head iceberg lettuce, thinly sliced**
- 1 **cup grated Monterey Jack or cheddar cheese**
- 2 **tomatoes, chopped**
- 1 **recipe Avocado Salsa (see next column)**

In a 3-quart saucepan, heat 2 tablespoons vegetable oil over medium heat. Add chicken tenders and cook for about 10 minutes or until cooked through. Add garlic and cook until fragrant, about 30 to 60 seconds. Add green chiles and sour cream; stir well. Cook over low heat until hot. Cover and set aside.

Generously brush tortillas with vegetable oil on both sides. Place a well-greased 10-inch skillet over medium heat. Fry flour tortillas, one at a time, for about 30 seconds on each side or until lightly browned and blistered. Remove from skillet and stack.

Arrange lettuce on each tortilla. Top with chicken mixture; sprinkle with cheese and tomato.

May also serve taco style. Spoon Avocado Salsa on top of tostados or in tacos and serve immediately. Makes 6 servings.

AVOCADO SALSA

- 3 **tablespoons vegetable oil**
- 2 **tablespoons lime or lemon juice**
- ½ **teaspoon sugar**
- ½ **teaspoon salt**
- 1 **avocado, peeled, pitted and chopped**
- 1 **tomato, chopped**

In a small bowl, combine all salsa ingredients and stir together. Cover and refrigerate for at least one hour.

Beef Fajitas

Just listen to the raves!

- 3 **pounds stir-fry beef**
- 2 **tablespoons vegetable oil, plus more for cooking tortillas**
- 1 **teaspoon salt**
- 1 **teaspoon pepper**
- 1 **onion, thinly sliced into rings**
- 1 **green bell pepper, sliced into strips**
- 1 **red bell pepper, sliced into strips**
- 3 **cloves garlic, minced**
  Juice of 1 lemon or 2 limes
- 12 **(6-inch) flour tortillas**
  Avocado, chopped
  Salsa
  Cheddar or Monterey Jack cheese, grated
  Sour cream

In a large skillet, stir-fry beef in hot oil over medium heat until cooked through, about 10 minutes. Sprinkle with salt and pepper. Add onion, peppers, garlic, and lemon or lime juice and cook for about 2 minutes. Cover and set aside.

Generously brush tortillas with vegetable oil on both sides. Place a well-greased 10-inch skillet over medium heat. Fry flour tortillas, one at a time, for about 30 seconds on each side or until lightly browned and blistered. Remove from skillet and stack.

Fill warmed tortillas with beef and vegetables. Add avocado, salsa, cheese, and sour cream, as desired. Serve immediately. Makes 12 fajitas.

Fiesta Rice

The whole crowd will like it.

- 3 **tablespoons olive oil**
- 1 **onion, chopped**
- 1 **clove garlic, minced**
- ½ **green pepper, chopped**
- 1 **cup long grain rice, uncooked**
- 1 **cup tomatoes, pureed**
- 1½ **cups chicken broth**

In a saucepan, heat olive oil over medium heat. Sauté onion, garlic, and green pepper until the onion is translucent. Add the rice and cook over low heat, stirring occasionally, until rice is golden. Add tomatoes and broth to rice; bring to a boil. Cover and simmer 20 minutes. Allow to stand 5 to 10 minutes before serving. Makes 8 servings.

HOW TO ROAST BELL PEPPERS

Many recipes call for roasted peppers. Follow these instructions for easy roasting.

4 red peppers, sliced in half lengthwise, cored and seeded
Olive oil

Preheat the broiler.

Lay the pepper pieces skin-side-up on a flat broiling pan and place the pan 3 to 4 inches below the heat. Broil the peppers for about 10 minutes until the skins are charred (they should be black). Remove peppers to a plastic bag, seal it with a twist tie, and set aside. Let the peppers steam in the bag for 15 minutes. Remove the peppers from the bag and slip off the charred skins. Place the peppers in a one quart storage jar. Add olive oil just to cover. Store, covered, in the refrigerator for up to a week.

Wedding Cookies

They're rich and sweet . . . cha cha cha!

- 1   **cup butter, softened**
- ½   **cup powdered sugar**
- 1   **teaspoon vanilla**
- ½   **teaspoon almond extract (optional)**
- 2   **cups flour**
- ¼   **teaspoon salt**
- 1   **cup pecans, chopped**
-     **Powdered sugar**

In a large bowl, cream together butter, sugar, vanilla extract, and almond extract, if using. In another bowl, combine flour and salt. Add to creamed mixture and mix well. Stir in pecans. Mix dough until it holds together. Form dough into 1-inch balls. Place on a greased baking sheet, about 2 inches apart. Bake at 400 degrees for 10 to 12 minutes or until lightly browned. Cool cookies for a few minutes and roll in powdered sugar several times until well coated. Makes about 3 dozen.

Fried Ice Cream

This dessert will make you want to do the Mexican Hat Dance!

- ½   **gallon vanilla ice cream**
- 2   **teaspoons cinnamon, plus some for topping**
- 3   **cups coarsely crushed cornflakes**
-     **Vegetable oil**
-     **Honey**
-     **Whipped cream, sweetened**

At least a day in advance, remove ice cream from freezer and thaw at room temperature for 10 minutes. Peel ice cream from carton. With a knife, cut ice cream in half and then fourths, making eight slices. Quickly shape into 8 balls. Sprinkle each ice cream ball with cinnamon and roll in crushed corn flakes. Place on a tray and freeze until very hard.

On serving day, place individual serving bowls in freezer to chill. Heat enough oil in deep frying pan to cover ice cream balls. Heat to 375 degrees and fry each ball one at a time for 3 to 5 seconds. Always use caution when deep frying. Top with honey, whipped cream, and a sprinkle of cinnamon. Serve immediately. Makes 8 ice cream balls.

MOTHER'S DAY BRUNCH

Make Mother's Day a time to honor Mother in some fabulous way, to "arise up, and call her blessed" (Proverbs 31:28). If fathers and children plan together, they are sure to come up with something wonderful to really please—and spoil—Mom. "God loveth a cheerful giver" (2 Corinthians 9:7), and with everyone helping happily, you can truly give a family "gift" from the heart.

The following brunch menu is as fresh as spring. Mom will enjoy Eggs Benedict Squares or the Deviled Eggs and Shrimp Dish. Both are easy favorites. Children can help stir together the beautiful Blueberry Muffins and help prepare bananas, strawberries, and grapes for refreshing Spring Fruit Cups. You'll bring a surprised smile to Mom's face when dessert is served. The Luscious Lemon Bundt Cake or Strawberry Frozen Squares look beautiful and taste terrific, and they are not hard to make. Whipping the egg whites for the strawberry dessert does take time but is worth it. Even if everything doesn't turn out perfectly, Mom will be grateful and happy for your efforts and love.

If family members play an instrument, a special musical number could be a wonderful beginning or ending to the dinner or brunch. Or, maybe the whole family could sing a special song for her. Homemade cards, poems, or notes are always treasured. Small children could help make cookies by tracing their hands on cookie dough. Photos from years past could be gathered as reminders of good times. New ones could be taken. Mother will undoubtedly appreciate the "royal treatment" on this special day.

Eggs Benedict Squares

Make Mom proud!

- 4 whole English muffins, split in half
- 2 cups grated cheddar cheese, divided
- 3 cups cooked and chopped broccoli or asparagus
- 1 cup chopped ham
- ½ cup chopped red pepper
- 8 eggs
- 2 cups milk
- 1 teaspoon dry mustard
- ¾ teaspoon salt
- ⅛ teaspoon pepper
- 1 recipe Hollandaise Sauce (see next column)

Place the muffin halves in a greased 9x13-inch baking dish. Sprinkle halves with 1 cup cheddar cheese, the cooked broccoli or asparagus, chopped ham, and red pepper. Beat eggs in a medium bowl; stir in milk, dry mustard, salt, and pepper. Pour egg mixture over muffins. Bake at 350 degrees for 35 minutes. Remove from oven. Top with remaining cheese. Bake an additional 5 to 10 minutes or until cheese is melted. Top with Hollandaise Sauce. Makes 8 servings.

HOLLANDAISE SAUCE

- 2 egg yolks
- 1 tablespoon lemon juice
- ½ cup butter, divided
- 1 or 2 drops Tabasco® sauce (optional)

In a saucepan, stir egg yolks and lemon juice vigorously until well mixed. Add ¼ cup butter. Place saucepan over low heat and stir mixture constantly with a wire whisk until butter is melted. Stir in remaining butter. Continue stirring vigorously until butter is melted and sauce is thickened. Stir in Tabasco sauce, if desired. Serve hot or at room temperature.

MOTHER'S DAY BRUNCH

Deviled Eggs and Shrimp Dish

Sinfully delicious!

6   hard-cooked eggs, peeled and sliced in half

1   tablespoon Miracle Whip® salad dressing

1   teaspoon mustard

1   cup fresh cooked medium shrimp

¼   cup butter

¼   cup flour

½   teaspoon salt

2   cups milk

1½   cups grated cheddar cheese

½   teaspoon Worcestershire sauce

1   teaspoon mustard

1   tablespoon grated onion

½   cup bread crumbs

2   tablespoons butter, melted

Remove yolks from hard-cooked eggs and place in a bowl; set aside whites to fill later. Add Miracle Whip and 1 teaspoon mustard to yolks and mash together with a fork. Spoon yolk mixture into egg whites. Arrange deviled eggs in greased 9x13-inch baking dish. Sprinkle with shrimp.

In a saucepan, melt butter over medium heat. Stir in flour and salt. Gradually add milk and stir until mixture reaches a boil. Cook and stir 2 more minutes. Remove from heat. Stir in cheddar cheese, Worcestershire Sauce, 1 teaspoon mustard, and grated onion. Spoon sauce over eggs and shrimp.

In a separate bowl, stir together bread crumbs and melted butter. Sprinkle crumbs over sauce. Bake at 325 degrees for about 10 minutes. Makes 6 servings.

Papa's Whole-Wheat Pancakes

The whole family will love them!

1   cup milk

1   cup whole-wheat flour

¼   cup sugar

2   eggs

¼   cup butter, melted

1   teaspoon baking soda

2   teaspoons baking powder

¼   teaspoon salt

Combine milk and flour and beat in a blender on high speed for 2 minutes. Add remaining ingredients and beat on high for 2 more minutes. Using a ¼-cup measuring cup, pour pancake batter on hot griddle and cook until lightly browned on both sides. Serve with butter and warm syrup. Makes about 12 pancakes.

Blueberry Muffins

These muffins are both fast and fabulous.

- 1½ **cups flour**
- ¼ **cup sugar**
- ¼ **cup brown sugar**
- 2 **teaspoons baking powder**
- ¼ **teaspoon salt**
- 1 **teaspoon cinnamon**
- 1 **egg, beaten**
- ½ **cup butter, melted**
- ½ **cup milk**
- 1 **teaspoon lemon zest**
- 1 **cup fresh or frozen blueberries**
- 1 **recipe Muffin Topping (see below)**
- 1 **recipe Muffin Glaze (see next column)**

In a large bowl, combine flour, sugar, brown sugar, baking powder, salt, and cinnamon. Stir until well blended. Make a well in center of mixture. Place egg, butter, and milk in center and stir just until blended. Carefully stir in lemon zest and blueberries. Fill 12 muffin cups. Sprinkle with Muffin Topping. Bake at 350 degrees for about 20 minutes. Remove from oven and drizzle with Muffin Glaze.

MUFFIN TOPPING

- ½ **cup pecans, chopped**
- ½ **cup packed brown sugar**
- ¼ **cup flour**
- 1 **teaspoon cinnamon**
- 1 **teaspoon lemon zest**
- 2 **tablespoons butter, melted**

In a bowl, combine above ingredients and sprinkle over muffins.

MUFFIN GLAZE

- ½ **cup powdered sugar**
- 1 **tablespoon fresh lemon juice**

In a bowl, mix powdered sugar and lemon juice together. Drizzle over muffins after baking.

Spring Fruit Cups

Treat Mom to the tastes of spring!

- 1 **(15-ounce) can mandarin oranges, undrained**
- 1 **cup strawberries, sliced**
- 1 **cup grapes, red or green**
- 2 **apples, chopped**
- 2 **bananas, sliced**
- 1 **cup orange juice**
- ¼ **cup sugar**

Combine all ingredients in a large bowl. Place in small cups when ready to serve. Makes about 8 cups.

Luscious Lemon Bundt Cake

This cake is fit for a queen!

  1   yellow cake mix
  1   small (3-ounce) package vanilla instant pudding mix
  4   eggs
  1   cup sour cream
  2   teaspoons vanilla
  ¾   cup vegetable oil
  1   recipe Lemon Sour Cream Sauce (see below)
      Fresh strawberries or raspberries

In a large bowl, combine all ingredients except sauce and mix well. Pour into a greased Bundt pan. Bake at 325 degrees for about 40 to 45 minutes. Serve topped with Lemon Sour Cream Sauce and fresh strawberries or raspberries. Makes about 10 servings.

LEMON SOUR CREAM SAUCE

  1   cup sour cream
  1   teaspoon grated lemon peel
  1   teaspoon lemon juice
  ½   cup powdered sugar

Combine all ingredients in a small bowl. Dollop on individual pieces of Luscious Lemon Bundt Cake.

Strawberry Frozen Squares

You'll hear the raves with these squares!

  1   cup flour
  ¼   cup packed brown sugar
  ½   cup chopped pecans
  ½   cup butter, melted
  2   egg whites
  1   cup sugar
  1   tablespoon lemon juice
  1   cup whipping cream, plus sugar to sweeten
  2   cups sliced strawberries, or 1 (10-ounce) package frozen strawberries

In a bowl, combine flour, brown sugar, pecans, and butter. Press mixture onto greased baking sheet. Bake at 350 degrees for about 8 to 10 minutes, or until golden brown; remove from oven and cool. With a fork, break crust into crumbs. Sprinkle half of the crumbs into a greased 9x13-inch pan. Set remaining half aside.

In a large bowl, beat egg whites on high speed for about 5 minutes. Gradually add sugar and lemon juice. Beat 3 minutes more; set aside. In another bowl, whip and sweeten cream, then use a hand mixer to mix strawberries and whipped cream together. Gently fold strawberry mixture into egg-white mixture; spoon evenly over crumbs. Sprinkle remaining crumbs over top. Freeze at least 6 hours before serving. Cut into squares. Makes about 12 servings.

Soft Sugar Cookies

Make as a gift for Mom.

½ **cup butter**

½ **cup margarine**

1 **egg**

1 **cup powdered sugar**

2 **cups flour**

½ **teaspoon salt**

½ **teaspoon cream of tartar**

½ **teaspoon baking soda**

1 **teaspoon vanilla**

1 **recipe Cream Cheese Frosting (see next column)**

In a large bowl cream butter and margarine together. Add egg and mix. Add powdered sugar and beat well. Add remaining ingredients, except frosting, and mix. On a floured surface, roll out dough about ¼-inch thick. Add additional flour if dough is too sticky. Cut dough into desired shapes. Bake on greased cookie sheets at 350 degrees for 10 to 12 minutes. Cool on wire rack and frost with Cream Cheese Frosting. Makes 2 to 3 dozen cookies.

CREAM CHEESE FROSTING

1 **(8-ounce) package cream cheese, softened**

½ **cup butter, melted**

4 **cups powdered sugar**

1 **teaspoon vanilla**

Cream the softened cream cheese; blend with butter. Add powdered sugar and vanilla and beat well.

A MEMORIAL DAY POTLUCK

Remembering is at the heart of Memorial Day. Families gather armfuls of fragrant roses, beautiful peonies, and stately purple and yellow irises from gardens. Glass jars are filled with delicate lilies of the valley, blue forget-me-nots, and bleeding hearts in remembrance of those who have gone before. Stories of other times and places are shared as families reach back to their roots. Sometimes there are visits to small towns as families have a chance to reconnect.

The weather is often beautiful at the end of May. A potluck dinner is the perfect way to share time together. As families arrive, fill up picnic tables with Chicken-Broccoli Casserole, South African Curried Beef, Potato Alfredo, Baked Asparagus, Russian Cream, Pineapple Upside-Down Cake, and any number of delicious recipes from other sections of this book. Disposable containers will be appreciated for easy cleanup. While waiting for the meal to begin, gather children together and share family photos, stories, or memories. You might want to read a short book together such as *Stone Soup*, which will help children understand the sense of family and community.

When it's finally time for supper, pull up a chair under a shady oak tree and let the relaxing celebration officially begin. You'll find that potlucks aren't just about sharing food; they're about spending time together.

Chicken-Broccoli Casserole

Remember this all-time favorite?

2 (10-ounce) packages frozen broccoli
   florets

6 chicken breasts, cooked and cubed
   Salt and pepper to taste

½ cup grated cheddar cheese

2 (10-ounce) cans cream of chicken soup

½ cup sour cream

1 teaspoon lemon juice

¼ teaspoon mild curry powder (optional)

1 cup bread crumbs

½ cup butter, melted

Cook broccoli according to package directions;
drain and place in greased 9x13-inch baking dish.
Place cooked and cubed chicken breasts over
broccoli. Lightly salt and pepper. Sprinkle with
cheese. In a bowl, stir together cream of chicken
soup, sour cream, lemon juice, and curry powder.
Spoon sauce evenly over broccoli, chicken, and
cheese. Place bread crumbs in a small bowl. Drizzle
butter over crumbs and gently stir to coat. Sprinkle
over sauce. Bake at 350 degrees for 25 to 30 minutes. Makes 8 servings.

Pork Chops in the Oven

Oh, so good!

6 pork chops

2 tablespoons vegetable oil or butter

1 cup chopped onion

2 (10-ounce) cans cream of mushroom
   soup

½ teaspoon dried sage (optional)

In a large skillet, brown pork chops in vegetable oil
or butter over medium heat for about 10 minutes.
Add onions and continue cooking for an additional
10 minutes. Remove pork chops from skillet and
place in a greased 9x13-inch baking dish. Pour soup
into skillet with onions and drippings. Add sage.
Stir and heat for about 5 minutes. Pour over pork
chops. Bake at 350 degrees for about 40 minutes.
Serve with rice or potatoes. Makes 6 servings.

South African Curried Beef

A surprisingly good combination!

2   pounds beef stew meat

2   tablespoons butter or olive oil

1   large onion, chopped

1   tomato, chopped

2   (10-ounce) cans beef consommé soup, undiluted

1   teaspoon salt

2   tablespoons mild curry powder

½   cup flour

1   cup water

¼   cup ketchup

1   recipe Chutney Sauce (see next column)
    Rice for 8
    Condiments, including coconut, peanuts, cubed bananas, chopped green onions

In a Dutch oven or large pot, brown beef in butter or olive oil. Add onion, tomatoes, beef consommé soup, and salt. Cover and cook at 350 degrees for about 1½ hours. Remove from oven. Stir in curry powder. In a bowl, whisk together flour and water, stirring until smooth. Add flour mixture to simmering meat to make gravy; stir until thickened. Add ketchup. Serve beef over rice. Place bowls of condiments on the table. Let each person top their rice and beef with condiments of their choice. Top with one or two tablespoons of Chutney Sauce per serving. Makes 6 to 8 servings.

CHUTNEY SAUCE

½   cup packed brown sugar

½   cup apricot preserves

2   tablespoons Worcestershire sauce

In a saucepan, combine brown sugar, apricot preserves and Worcestershire sauce. Heat and stir until the sugar is dissolved. Serve over curried beef. This sauce may be made in advance and stored in the refrigerator. This is also good over ham.

Chicken Pasta Salad

Try it; you'll like it!

4   cups bow-tie pasta

4   cups cooked and cubed chicken

½   cup chopped green onions

1   cup sliced water chestnuts (optional)

1   (20-ounce) can pineapple tidbits, drained

1½ cups mayonnaise

¼   cup red wine vinegar

2   teaspoons salt

½   teaspoon pepper

2   cups red grapes

1   cup pecans, coarsely chopped

½   cup Craisins®

Cook pasta according to package directions; drain. In a large bowl, combine all ingredients except grapes, pecans, and Craisins. Marinate mixture in refrigerator for several hours or overnight. Add grapes, pecans, and Craisins just before serving. Makes about 12 cups.

Potato Alfredo

They'll be coming back for more of this.

- 8 **potatoes, peeled and cut in thick strips (French-fry style)**
- 1 **cup chopped onion**
- 2 **tablespoons butter, melted**
- 1 **tablespoon salt**
- 2 **teaspoons dried thyme**
- 4 **cloves garlic, minced, or 2 teaspoons garlic salt**
- 1 **cup freshly grated Parmesan cheese**
- 2 **cups cream or half-and-half**

Place potato strips in a large baking dish. Combine all other ingredients in a medium bowl; pour over potatoes. Bake uncovered at 400 degrees for about 1 hour or until potatoes are tender. Makes about 8 servings.

Baked Asparagus

Beautiful!

- 2 **pounds fresh asparagus**
- ¼ **cup butter, melted and divided**
- ½ **cup sour cream**
- ½ **cup bread crumbs**

Trim woody ends from asparagus and discard. Cook asparagus in a large pot of boiling water until crisp-tender, about 3 minutes. Drain. Rinse asparagus under cold water; drain well. Place in a shallow greased baking dish. Spoon 2 tablespoons melted butter over top. Spread with sour cream. In a bowl, combine bread crumbs and remaining 2 tablespoons melted butter. Sprinkle over top of asparagus dish. Bake at 325 degrees for about 10 minutes. Makes 4 to 6 servings.

Copper Penny Carrots

You can "count" on these.

- 2 **pounds carrots (6 cups)**
- 1 **(10-ounce) can tomato soup**
- ½ **cup sugar**
- ½ **cup vegetable oil**
- 1 **teaspoon salt**
- 1 **teaspoon mustard**
- ½ **cup vinegar**
- 1 **onion, sliced in thin rings**
- 1 **green bell pepper, cut in thin strips**

Peel and slice carrots. In a large pot, cook carrots in a small amount of water until tender-crisp; set aside. In a saucepan, combine tomato soup, sugar, vegetable oil, salt, mustard, and vinegar. Bring to a boil. Combine carrots, onions, and green peppper. Pour hot dressing over vegetables. Stir together. Refrigerate overnight. Serve warm or cold. Will keep for a week in the refrigerator. Makes 12 servings.

Peanut Butter Cookies

They'll disappear!

- 1   cup butter or margarine
- 1   cup sugar
- 1   cup packed brown sugar
- 2   eggs
- 1   cup peanut butter
- 1   teaspoon vanilla
- 3   cups flour
- 2   teaspoons baking soda
- ¼   teaspoon salt
-     Sugar
-     Hershey's® candy kisses (optional)

In a bowl, cream together butter or margarine, sugar, brown sugar, eggs, peanut butter, and vanilla. In a separate bowl, stir together flour, baking soda, and salt; add to creamed mixture and beat together. Roll dough into 1½-inch balls and roll in sugar. Bake at 375 degrees for 8 to 10 minutes. While still warm, place Hershey's candy kiss on top, if desired. Makes 5 dozen cookies.

Russian Cream

Fabulously rich! Have a slice with fresh berries.

- ¾   cup sugar
- 1   envelope Knox® gelatin
- ½   cup water
- 1   cup whipping cream
- 1½   cups sour cream
- 1   teaspoon vanilla
- 2   cups sliced strawberries, raspberries, or blueberries

In a large saucepan, combine sugar, gelatin, and water. Mix well, then let stand for 5 minutes. Bring mixture to a full boil, stirring constantly. Remove from heat and allow to cool. Pour in whipping cream; set aside. In a large bowl, blend sour cream and vanilla. Gradually beat in sugar mixture with a wire whisk until mixture is smooth. Place in a greased mold or pie plate. Cover and chill overnight or at least 4 hours. Top with fresh berries. Serves 6.

Toll House Pie

Terrific! You'll be surprised how easy it is to make.

- ½ **cup sugar**
- ½ **cup packed brown sugar**
- 1 **cup butter, melted**
- 2 **eggs**
- ½ **cup flour**
- 1 **cup chocolate chips**
- 1 **cup chopped pecans**
- 1 **pie crust**
    Whipped cream, sweetened
    Ice cream, if desired

Combine sugars in a large bowl; add melted butter, eggs, and flour. Beat until well mixed. Batter will be thin. Stir in chocolate chips and pecans. Place in a 9-inch pie crust (may use a frozen crust). Place on a baking sheet and bake at 325 degrees for 50 to 60 minutes. Top with whipped cream or ice cream to serve. Makes 6 servings.

Chocolate Truffle Cheesecake

Fabulous! Make a day ahead.

- 1 **recipe Chocolate Crumb Crust (see next column)**
- 1 **(11-ounce) package chocolate chips**
- 3 **(8-ounce) packages cream cheese, softened**
- 1 **(14-ounce) can sweetened condensed milk**
- 4 **eggs**
- 2 **teaspoons vanilla**
    Fresh raspberries or strawberries as garnish

Prepare Chocolate Crumb Crust; set aside. Melt chocolate chips in microwave on high power for 1 minute; stir. Microwave 20 seconds more and stir until well blended; set aside. In a large mixing bowl, beat cream cheese until fluffy. Gradually beat in sweetened condensed milk and melted chocolate. Add eggs and vanilla and beat until smooth. Pour into prepared Chocolate Crumb Crust. Bake at 300 degrees for about 1 hour or until center is set. Cool, then chill in refrigerator overnight. To serve, garnish with fresh raspberries or strawberries. Makes 12 servings.

CHOCOLATE CRUMB CRUST

- 1½ **cups vanilla wafer crumbs**
- ½ **cup powdered sugar**
- ⅓ **cup unsweetened cocoa**
- ½ **cup butter or margarine, melted**

Combine all ingredients in a medium bowl. Press firmly on bottom of greased 9-inch springform pan.

Pineapple Upside-Down Cake

A wonderful old favorite.

  1   **cup packed brown sugar**
  1½   **cup butter, softened and divided**
  1   **(20-ounce) can pineapple rings,**
       drained with juice reserved
  2   **cups sugar**
  1   **tablespoon vanilla**
  2   **eggs**
  2¼   **cups flour**
  1   **teaspoon baking soda**
  ½   **teaspoon salt**
       Whipped cream (optional)

Combine brown sugar and ½ cup butter; spread on bottom of greased 9x13-inch pan. Place pineapple rings on top. Cream the remaining 1 cup butter with sugar. Add vanilla and eggs and beat well. In a separate bowl, stir together flour, baking soda, and salt. Add to creamed mixture. Beat in 1 cup of the reserved pineapple juice. Pour batter over pineapple rings and bake at 350 degrees for about 45 minutes, until toothpick inserted in center comes out clean. Cool slightly, serve warm. To serve, flip individual cake pieces over to show pineapple. Top with whipped cream if desired. Makes 12 servings.

SUMMER

COMING HOME

The excitement felt by those coming home is matched only by the joyful anticipation of those awaiting their return. Coming home is always a cause for celebration, whether the person returning is a missionary, military serviceman or woman, a college student, or a new mom coming home from the hospital. "A merry heart doeth good like a medicine" (Proverbs 17:22).

Familiar sights, sounds, and smells will be welcomed by someone who's been away. A homemade meal of family favorites is sure to please. The aromas will stir memories that say, "I'm home." There's nothing quite like Mom's Chicken and Dumplings or Beef Cubed Steaks with Potatoes and Gravy for real comfort food, and they'll love Feather-Light Overnight Rolls (see recipe on page 42). Cookies-and-Cream Cheesecake, Peach-Berry Dessert, or Heavenly Chocolate Pie all provide happy endings and elicit that old, familiar saying: "There's no place like home."

MENU ONE

Mom's Chicken and Dumplings

Welcome home! Chicken can be prepared a day in advance and refrigerated.

4	**chicken breasts, bone in**
4	**chicken thighs, bone in**
4	**cups water**
½	**cup chopped onion**
1	**tablespoon salt**
1	**cup chopped celery**
1½	**cups water**
1¼	**cups baby carrots**
3	**cups Bisquick®**
1	**cup milk**
¾	**cup frozen peas**

Place chicken breasts, chicken thighs, 4 cups water, onion, salt, and celery in a heavy 4- or 5-quart cooking pot; bring to a boil. Reduce heat to medium, cover, and simmer for 15 minutes. Turn off heat and let stand for 1 hour. Remove chicken from broth and set aside. When chicken is cool enough to handle, remove skin and bones from chicken and discard. Cut chicken into 2-inch pieces and return to broth. Add 1½ cups water and heat broth to boiling. Add carrots; simmer over low heat for 5 minutes. In a bowl, stir Bisquick and milk together to form a soft dough. With a large spoon, drop dumpling dough onto boiling broth, forming about ten dumplings. Reduce heat to medium. Simmer uncovered for 10 minutes. Cover and simmer for an additional 10 minutes. Sprinkle peas over the top of stew and cook just until heated through. Serve immediately. Makes 6 to 8 servings.

Fresh Asparagus

Willowy and wonderful!

2	**pounds fresh asparagus**
	Butter
	Salt

Trim woody ends from asparagus and discard. Cook asparagus in a large pot of boiling, salted water until crisp-tender, about 3 minutes. Drain. Rinse asparagus under cold water. Drain well. Butter and salt to taste. Makes 6 servings.

Apricot Set Salad

This salad has just the right tartness.

1 large (30-ounce) can apricot halves, drained with juice reserved

1 large (6-ounce) package orange Jell-O®

6 ounces frozen orange juice concentrate, thawed

1 tablespoon lemon juice

1 cup 7-Up®

6 to 8 purple lettuce leaves

In a small saucepan, bring 1½ cups of the reserved apricot juice to a boil over medium heat. Remove from heat. Add orange Jell-O and stir until dissolved; set aside. In a blender, process apricot halves, orange juice concentrate, and lemon juice until smooth. Add Jell-O mixture and 7-Up. Mix well. Pour in a greased 8x8-inch dish. Chill until firm. Cut salad in squares and place on purple lettuce leaves on individual plates. Makes about 6 to 8 servings.

Cookies-and-Cream Cheesecake

You'll get requests for this recipe.

3 cups finely crushed Oreo® cookies (36 cookies) divided

⅓ cup butter or margarine, melted

2 (8-ounce) packages cream cheese, softened

⅔ cup sugar

1 tablespoon vanilla

1 cup whipping cream, plus sugar to sweeten

Chocolate bar shavings, for garnish

In a bowl, stir together the 2 cups crushed Oreos and butter or margarine. Press into the bottom of a 9-inch pie plate or springform pan. Freeze or refrigerate until firm.

In a large bowl, beat cream cheese until fluffy. Gradually add sugar and vanilla. Blend well. Whip and sweeten cream; fold whipped cream and remaining 1 cup crushed Oreos into cream cheese mixture. Spoon into chilled crust. Refrigerate at least 2 hours before serving. Garnish with chocolate bar shavings. Makes about 6 to 8 servings.

Peach-Berry Dessert

This family favorite can bubble in the oven during dinner.

3   (15-ounce) cans sliced peaches, drained
½   teaspoon almond extract
    Juice of 1 lemon
1½ cups fresh or frozen blueberries, black-berries, or boysenberries
¾   cup butter or margarine, melted
1   cup flour
1¼ cups packed brown sugar
1¼ cups quick Quaker® Oats
    Vanilla ice cream

Place peaches in a 9x13-inch baking dish. Stir in almond extract and lemon juice. Sprinkle berries on top. In a bowl, combine butter or margarine, flour, brown sugar, and oats. Sprinkle over top of peaches. Bake at 350 degrees for 35 to 40 minutes. Serve warm with ice cream. Makes about 8 servings.

Note: Similar amounts of fresh, frozen, or bottled peaches in place of canned peaches are wonderful in this recipe.

MENU TWO

Beef Cubed Steaks with Potatoes and Gravy

They'll love this comfort food.

3   pounds ground beef
2   tablespoons butter or vegetable oil
1   onion, chopped
2   large (26-ounce) cans cream of mush-room soup
8   potatoes

Form ground beef into 8 thick square patties. In a large skillet, melt butter or oil over medium heat. Brown patties for about 10 minutes on each side. Add onion and continue cooking over medium heat for 5 minutes. Place patties, onions, and drippings in a greased 9x13-inch baking dish. Spoon cream of mushroom soup over top. Cover with loose foil. Wrap potatoes in foil and place on a baking sheet. Bake Beef Cubed Steaks and potatoes at 350 degrees for 1½ hours. To serve, spoon gravy from cooked steaks over baked potatoes. Makes 8 servings.

Glazed Carrots and Peas

A family favorite.

8   carrots, cut on bias ½-inch thick
1   tablespoon sugar
1   teaspoon cornstarch
¼   cup orange juice
2   tablespoons butter
1   (10-ounce) package frozen peas
    Salt to taste

Place carrots in a saucepan. Fill with water just to cover. Cook over medium heat for about 8 minutes, until tender but firm. Drain water from carrots; sprinkle carrots with sugar and cornstarch. Add orange juice and butter. Stir over low heat until thickened. Prepare peas according to package directions. Mix together with carrots. Salt to taste. Makes 8 servings.

Creamy Pineapple Lime Jell-O

Brings back memories.

2   cups water
1   large (6-ounce) package lime Jell-O®
2   tablespoons lime or lemon juice
1   (8-ounce) package cream cheese, softened
1   cup whipping cream, plus sugar to sweeten
1   (20-ounce) can crushed pineapple, undrained

In a saucepan, bring water to a boil. Remove from heat and dissolve Jell-O. Stir in lime or lemon juice. Refrigerate until syrupy. While Jell-O is in the refrigerator, beat cream cheese until smooth. Whip and sweeten cream. Fold whipped cream into cream cheese. Stir in crushed pineapple. Add cream cheese mixture to lime Jell-O and whisk together. Pour into an 8x8-inch dish. Refrigerate several hours until set. Makes 8 servings.

Heavenly Chocolate Pie

Light and luscious!

2   **cups crushed chocolate cookies**

⅓   **cup butter, melted**

2   **(6-ounce) Hershey's® chocolate bars**

1   **teaspoon vanilla**

1   **teaspoon salt**

1   **(12-ounce) carton frozen whipped topping, thawed**

    Whipped cream

Combine crushed cookies and butter. Press into a greased 9-inch pie plate. Freeze or refrigerate until firm. Break Hershey chocolate bars into pieces. Place in a medium bowl and microwave on high for 1 minute. Stir chocolate. Microwave for 30 seconds more. Stir and cool to room temperature. Add vanilla and salt. Whisk in thawed whipped topping. Pour into pie pan and chill for several hours. Top each serving with a dollop of whipped cream. Makes 8 servings.

A GRADUATION LUAU

After years of hard work, graduates deserve to hear, "Congratulations! You did it!" How about honoring the graduate with a luau? Celebrate island-style, and bring your graduate's dreams of paradise—ocean breezes, tropical flowers, and fabulous food—to life. Seashells, tiki torches, and exotic blossoms as decorations will enhance the mood.

Depending on the schedule of graduation events, the celebration could be the same day or another day. But whenever it is, make sure the occasion is relaxing and festive. The party can be simple or elaborate. If you have time and the budget, stop at a local party shop for leis, island music, and tropical flowers to tuck behind an ear.

Then let the feast begin. Serve some or all of the dishes suggested in this menu. The Sweet-and-Sour Pork is sensational and the Polynesian Chicken Salad is full of flavor and crunch. Marine cuisine is delicious and healthy and can be surprisingly simple to prepare. You might also look to another recipe in this book and serve Baked Salmon or Halibut Fillets (see the recipe on page 26). You may want to stir-fry seafood with vegetables, skewer scallops and shrimp for the barbecue, or prepare seafood Caesar by adding crab, shrimp, or salmon to your favorite Caesar salad recipe.

Fresh fruit is always devoured. Add papaya, mango, or other exotic fruits to the Fresh Fruit Platter on page 82 for another great menu idea. The Shrimp in Shells is sumptuous and the Whole Salmon spectacular. Everyone will be in paradise when Coconut Cream Dessert is served. Your guests will agree: "He that is of a merry heart hath a continual feast" (Proverbs 15:15). Aloha!

Sweet-and-Sour Pork

Enjoy this island favorite.

2   tablespoons butter

2   tablespoons olive oil

3   pounds lean pork, cut in strips

¼   cup cornstarch

2   teaspoons salt

1   teaspoon pepper

½   cup packed brown sugar

½   cup vinegar

2   (20-ounce) cans pineapple tidbits, drained with juice reserved

2   tablespoons soy sauce

1½   cups red or green bell pepper, cut in strips

½   cup thinly sliced onion
    Rice for 8 to 10

Melt butter in a large skillet; add olive oil. Stir-fry pork strips until browned, about 10 minutes. Cover and simmer on low for about 30 minutes. Drain meat and set aside.

In same skillet, combine cornstarch, salt, pepper, brown sugar, vinegar, 2 cups of the reserved pineapple juice, and soy sauce. Cook and stir until mixture comes to a boil. Reduce heat. Stir and cook 2 minutes. Add hot pork, peppers, sliced onion, and pineapple tidbits. Cook 3 minutes longer over medium heat. Serve over rice. Makes 8 to 10 servings.

Shrimp in Shells

Seashells can be purchased at a specialty cooking store.

7   tablespoons butter, divided

1   cup sliced fresh mushrooms

2   tablespoons thinly sliced green onion

1   clove garlic, minced

¼   cup flour

1   cup half-and-half

½   cup white grape juice or apple juice

1   tablespoon fresh lemon juice

½   teaspoon salt

2   pounds fresh cooked shrimp

½   cup bread crumbs

1   tablespoon butter, melted
    Parsley, for garnish

8   seashells

In a skillet, melt 3 tablespoons butter. Sauté mushrooms, onions, and garlic in butter for about 2 minutes; set aside. In a saucepan, melt 4 tablespoons butter. Stir in flour until well blended. Add half and half, white grape juice or apple juice, lemon juice, and salt. Stir over medium heat until mixture comes to a boil. Cook and stir about 2 more minutes. Remove from heat and stir in shrimp. Spoon into large seashells. Stir together bread crumbs and melted butter; sprinkle over each seashell. Bake at 350 degrees for about 10 minutes. Garnish with parsley. Makes about 8 servings.

Polynesian Chicken Salad

Wontons can be made ahead. They add flavor and flair!

½   (12-ounce) package wontons

1   head lettuce, shredded

2   cups cooked and cubed chicken

4   green onions, chopped

2   tablespoons toasted sesame seeds

4   stalks celery, chopped

1   recipe Polynesian Salad Dressing (see below)

Cut each wonton square into four strips. Fry according to package directions; set aside. (Use caution when deep frying.) In a bowl, combine lettuce, chicken, onions, sesame seeds, and celery. Just before serving, toss with desired amount of Polynesian Salad Dressing and top with fried wonton strips. Makes 8 to 10 servings.

POLYNESIAN SALAD DRESSING

4   tablespoons sugar

2   teaspoons salt

½   teaspoon pepper

4   tablespoons vinegar

1   tablespoon soy sauce

½   cup vegetable oil

¼   teaspoon sesame seed oil

Combine all ingredients and mix well. Refrigerate for several hours before serving.

Roasted Salmon with Cucumber Sauce

Sensational!

1   (4-pound) whole salmon

2   lemons, sliced

1   onion, sliced

4   sprigs fresh dill weed (optional)

1   bunch fresh thyme (optional)

1   recipe Cucumber Sauce (see next page)

Choose a whole cleaned fresh salmon. Place lemon and onion slices, dill, and thyme inside salmon. Line a roasting pan with aluminum foil or parchment paper; grease well with cooking spray. Place salmon in roasting pan; cover loosely with foil. Bake at 350 degrees for about 1 hour or until cooked through. Serve with Cucumber Sauce. Makes about 12 servings.

CUCUMBER SAUCE

- 1 **cup sour cream**
- 1 **cup mayonnaise**
- 2 **medium cucumbers, peeled, seeded, and cut into very thin slices**
- 1 **tablespoon grated onion**
- 1 **tablespoon chopped fresh dill weed (or 1 teaspoon dried dill weed)**
- ½ **teaspoon salt**
- ¼ **teaspoon pepper**

Stir together sour cream and mayonnaise. Stir in cucumbers, onion, dill weed, salt, and pepper. Refrigerate at least four hours before serving.

Coconut Cream Dessert

It's paradise!

- 1 **cup flour**
- 2 **tablespoons sugar**
- ½ **cup cold butter**
- ½ **cup chopped pecans**
- 1 **(8-ounce) package cream cheese, softened**
- 1 **cup powdered sugar**
- 2 **cups whipping cream, plus sugar to sweeten**
- 4 **cups milk**
- 3 **(3-ounce) packages coconut cream instant pudding mix**
- ½ **cup flaked coconut**

To prepare crust, combine flour and the 2 tablespoons sugar in a medium bowl. Cut in butter until crumbly. Stir in pecans. Press mixture into a greased 9x13-inch baking dish. Bake at 325 degrees for 20 to 25 minutes or until edges are lightly browned.

Beat cream cheese and powdered sugar in a small bowl until smooth. Whip and sweeten cream. Fold half of whipped cream into cream cheese mixture. Spread over the crust. In a bowl, whisk milk and pudding mixes for 2 minutes. Let stand for 2 minutes or until soft-set. Spread over cream cheese mixture. Top with remaining whipped cream.

Toast coconut by spreading it on a large baking sheet and toasting at 325 degrees for about 5 minutes or until lightly browned. Sprinkle over dessert. Refrigerate overnight. Makes 12 to 16 servings.

FATHER'S DAY DINNER

Good food, lovingly prepared, can go a long way in showing gratitude on Dad's special day. So surprise him with this easy and hearty dinner fit for a king: Beef Stroganoff is sure to please; Green Beans with Bacon makes for a grand side dish; melt-in-your-mouth cheesy Onion Bread will be ready in minutes. If weather permits, serve the meal outside and add to the joy.

Children can help prepare and arrange gorgeous fruits of the season for the Fresh Fruit Platter: melons in colors of the rainbow, fresh pineapple, glorious grapes, piles of bright red strawberries, and fresh green mint from the garden. Children can also help make the marvelous Mississippi Mud Pie with caramel topping (a Dad's kind of dessert). Some notes of appreciation or precious artwork will bring a smile to Dad's face. Make some treasured memories.

Beef Stroganoff

Fit for a king!

1½ **pounds top round steak, sliced about ¼-inch thick**

4 **tablespoons flour**

2 **teaspoons salt**

½ **teaspoon pepper**

6 **tablespoons butter, divided**

1½ **cups chopped onion**

1 **clove garlic, minced**

2 **tablespoons olive oil**

1 **(10 ½ ounce) can beef consommé**

1 **pound fresh mushrooms or 1 (8-ounce) can mushrooms**

1 **tablespoon Worcestershire sauce**

½ **cup sour cream**

Noodles or rice for 8

Cut round-steak slices into strips about 1 inch wide and 2 inches long. Combine flour, salt, and pepper in a paper lunch sack or plastic bag. Add meat strips and shake until well coated. In a large frying pan, melt 4 tablespoons of the butter. Add onion and garlic and cook until lightly browned. Place in a bowl and set aside. In frying pan, melt remaining 2 tablespoons butter over medium heat. Add olive oil. Place meat strips in pan and brown on all sides. Add beef consommé and onion and garlic mixture. Cover and simmer over low heat for about 30 minutes. Add mushrooms and Worcestershire sauce and continue cooking until meat is tender, about 10 minutes. May be made a day ahead and reheated over low heat.

Just before serving, top with sour cream. Serve over buttered noodles or rice. Makes 8 servings.

Green Beans with Bacon

Dad will love these!

2 **(16-ounce) packages frozen green beans**

1 **pound bacon**

1 **onion, chopped**

¼ **cup vinegar**

¼ **cup sugar**

Salt and pepper to taste

Cook beans according to package directions; drain and set aside. In skillet, cook bacon. Remove bacon from skillet. Pour off bacon drippings, leaving about 3 tablespoons in skillet. Sauté onion in bacon drippings until tender. Add vinegar, sugar, and green beans. Stir together and heat through. Salt and pepper to taste. Place in serving dish. Crumble bacon over top and serve. Makes 12 servings.

Quick Onion Bread

It melts in your mouth.

2 cups finely chopped onion
¼ cup butter
2 cups grated cheddar cheese
2 eggs, beaten
1 cup milk
2⅔ cups Bisquick®
¼ cup butter, melted
2 teaspoons poppy seeds

Sauté onion in ¼ cup butter over medium heat about 3 minutes; set aside to cool. Mix cheese, eggs, and milk in a medium bowl. Add sautéed onions. Gently stir in Bisquick. Place dough in a greased 9x13-inch pan. Spoon ¼ cup melted butter over surface and sprinkle with poppy seeds. Bake at 425 degrees for about 25 minutes, until golden brown. Cool and cut into squares. Makes 12 servings.

Fresh Fruit Platter with Fruit Dip

Celebrate the tastes of summer.

1 head romaine lettuce
1 small cantaloupe
1 small honeydew melon
1 fresh pineapple
1 pint basket strawberries
8 red grape clusters
  Fresh Fruit Dip (see below)

Wash and separate romaine lettuce leaves and place on eight serving plates or 1 large platter. Cut cantaloupe and honeydew melons in half. Remove seeds and cut each melon into eight wedges. Remove peel. Cut pineapple into eight wedges. Remove skin. Arrange all fruit on top of lettuce leaves. Serve with Fresh Fruit Dip. Makes 8 servings.

FRESH FRUIT DIP

1 cup sour cream
1 cup packed brown sugar
1 tablespoon lemon juice

Stir together and serve with fresh fruit.

Mississippi Mud Pie

You can bank on it.

- 1 (15-ounce) package Oreo® cookies, crushed
- ¼ cup butter, melted
- ½ gallon burnt almond fudge or chocolate ice cream, softened
- 1 (12-ounce) tub nondairy frozen whipped topping, thawed to room temperature
- 1 small jar chocolate or caramel sauce, for topping
  Whipped cream
- 1 (1.55-ounce) Hershey's® chocolate bar, grated, for garnish
- 1 (8-ounce) bag toffee bits, for garnish

Mix crushed cookie crumbs with butter and press into a greased 9- or 10-inch pie pan to form a crust. Chill or freeze until firm.

In a large bowl, combine softened ice cream and whipped topping. Stir until well blended. Pour over chilled crust. Freeze overnight or for several hours.

When ready to serve, spoon desired amount of chocolate or caramel topping over individual servings. Add a dollop of whipped cream, grated chocolate, and toffee bits to garnish. Makes about 8 servings.

FOURTH OF JULY BARBECUE

Everyone from the littlest flag-waver to the old-timer loves the Fourth of July. Parades, fireworks, kids playing in the park, decorated bikes and wagons, flags flying, food, and fun are all happy images of Independence Day. For many, a Fourth of July barbecue is as much a tradition as parades and fireworks.

Enjoy food that matches the mood; nothing says "summer" like the smoky aroma and snappy sizzle of the barbecue. Though it's tempting to grill everything in sight, grilling only a couple of items for a dinner is usually a realistic goal. The Beef Flank Steaks and Teriyaki Chicken suggested in this menu are both perfect choices. If you choose to barbecue corn in husks, then you may want to oven-broil the Texas Toast to ensure room on the grill. If you have a garden, it's a great time to slice up those beautiful home-grown tomatoes and zucchini. After dinner, let the kids have fun making and eating Handmade Ice Cream.

Experiment with the menu, adding your own ideas and specialties. Get ready for a fabulous night of fireworks, whether you're viewing them from a patio, porch, or park. Seize the moment!

Beef Flank Steaks

Just smell that smoky goodness.

4   flank steaks
1   cup 7-Up®
½   cup soy sauce
½   cup vegetable oil
¼   teaspoon garlic powder
     Salt and pepper to taste
1   recipe Barbecue Sauce
     (see next column)

Place flank steaks in large Ziploc bags. In medium bowl, combine 7-Up, soy sauce, vegetable oil, and garlic powder. Add to Ziploc bags to cover steak. Refrigerate marinated steaks for at least 4 hours or overnight, turning occasionally. Drain steaks well, reserving marinade. Cook on greased grill over medium-hot coals or on medium-high setting, brushing often with marinade. Cook for about 4 to 6 minutes per side or until desired doneness. Steaks may also be broiled in the oven for 7 to 8 minutes per side. Season steaks with salt and pepper to taste. Cut diagonally across the grain in thin slices. Pass Barbecue Sauce. Makes about 12 servings.

BARBECUE SAUCE

2   cups ketchup
1½ cups packed brown sugar
¼   cup red wine vinegar
¼   cup Worcestershire sauce
¼   teaspoon Tabasco® sauce
⅛   teaspoon liquid smoke (available
     at the supermarket)

Combine all ingredients in a medium saucepan. Cook and stir over medium heat for about 5 minutes.

Teriyaki Chicken

Taste that terrific flavor!

6   boneless, skinless chicken breasts
½   cup soy sauce
½   cup packed brown sugar
½   teaspoon garlic salt

Place chicken in a large bowl. In a small bowl, combine soy sauce, brown sugar, and garlic salt. Pour over chicken. Stir to coat. Grill and turn over medium heat for about 20 minutes or until cooked through. May also be baked in the oven at 350 degrees for about 45 minutes. Makes 6 servings.

Grilled Corn on the Cob

Shucks, it's good!

12   ears of corn, with husks
½   cup butter or margarine, softened
1   teaspoon onion salt
     Salt and pepper to taste

Heat coals or gas grill to medium heat. Remove outer larger husks from each ear of corn. Turn back inner husks and remove silk. In bowl, combine butter or margarine and onion salt. Spread each ear of corn with onion butter. Reserve remaining onion butter. Pull inner husks back up over corn. Tie with fine wire or twist tie to secure. Grill corn, with grill uncovered, about 3 inches from heat for about 20 to 30 minutes. Turn corn frequently until tender. Serve with remaining onion butter. Makes 12 servings.

Pasta Vegetable Salad

Perfect for a celebration.

1   pound corkscrew pasta
1   Bermuda onion, thinly sliced into rings
1   large red bell pepper, thinly sliced
2   carrots, thinly sliced
1   head cauliflower, separated into small florets
2   cups broccoli florets
2   small zucchini, thinly sliced
½   pound fresh mushrooms, halved
1   (0.7-ounce) Good Seasons® Italian Dressing mix
1   (16-ounce) Bernstein's® Cheese and Garlic Italian dressing

Cook pasta according to package directions. Drain and rinse in cold water; set aside. Place washed and cut vegetables in a large bowl. Stir in pasta. Sprinkle with dry Italian dressing mix. Pour Cheese and Garlic Italian dressing over top. Toss and refrigerate overnight. Makes 12 servings.

Texas Toast on the Grill

It's thick and rustic.

- ¾ **cup butter or margarine, softened**
- 2   **teaspoons seasoned salt or garlic salt**
- 12 **slices Texas toast bread**

Heat coals or gas grill. Brush grill rack with vegetable oil. In a small bowl, stir together butter or margarine and seasoned or garlic salt. Spread on both sides of bread slices. Grill bread, uncovered, 4 inches from medium heat 4 to 6 minutes, turning once, until golden brown. Makes 12 servings.

Shrimp Boats

Set sail!

- 12 **hard-cooked eggs**
- 3   **tablespoons Miracle Whip® salad dressing**

     Salt and pepper to taste
- 1   **cup fresh tiny shrimp**
- 3   **slices cheese (1 ounce each, individually wrapped)**

     Toothpicks

Peel eggs and slice in half lengthwise. Remove yolk and mash with a fork in a small bowl. Blend yolks, Miracle Whip, and salt and pepper to taste. Fill egg whites with yolk mixture. Sprinkle tiny shrimp over eggs. Cut each cheese slice into 8 triangles. Push toothpick through cheese "sails" and place one in each egg half to make your boats. Makes 24 shrimp boats.

Fruit Cups

Enjoy fabulous fresh fruit!

- 4   **cups cubed cantaloupe**
- 2   **cups cubed honeydew melon**
- 1   **cup red grapes, cut in half**
- 2   **cups strawberries, sliced**
- ½   **cup sugar**
- 1   **tablespoon lemon juice**

Place fruit in a serving bowl. Stir together sugar and lemon juice. Gently pour over fruit and toss. Serve in individual cups. Makes about 12 servings.

FOURTH OF JULY BARBECUE

Flag Cake

You'll be proud!

- 1   package white cake mix
- 1¼ cups water
- ⅓   cup vegetable oil
- 3   eggs
- 1   recipe Cream Cheese Frosting (see below)
- ½   cup blueberries
- 2   pints (4 cups) strawberries, stems removed and sliced in half

Make cake according to package directions, using water, oil, and eggs as listed above. Pour batter into a greased 9x13-inch baking dish. Bake at 350 degrees for 30 to 35 minutes. Cool. Frost with Cream Cheese Frosting. Decorate with fruit just before serving. For flag design, arrange blueberries on upper-left corner of frosted cake to create stars. Arrange strawberries in four rows over frosted cake to create stripes. Serve immediately. Makes 12 to 15 servings.

CREAM CHEESE FROSTING

- 1   (8-ounce) package cream cheese, softened
- ½   cup butter, melted
- 4   cups powdered sugar

Cream the softened cream cheese. Blend with butter. Add powdered sugar and beat well.

Handmade Ice Cream

Children will love this after-dinner activity.

- 1   cup milk
- 1   cup half-and-half
- ½   teaspoon vanilla extract
- ½   cup sugar
- 1   cup fresh or frozen strawberries or raspberries (optional)
- 1   quart-size Ziploc® bag
- 1   gallon-size Ziploc® bag
       Duct tape
- 2   pounds crushed ice or ice cubes
- 1   cup coarse rock salt
- ½   cup water
       Towel

In a medium bowl, mix together milk, half-and-half, vanilla, and sugar. If adding fruit, mix all ingredients in blender. Pour mixture into a quart-size Ziploc bag. Squeeze out excess air and seal with duct tape. Put the quart-size bag into the gallon-size bag and fill the gallon bag with ice, salt, and water. Squeeze excess air out of bag and seal with duct tape. Toss the bag up and down for about 10 minutes. Use a hand towel to prevent hands from getting cold. When ice cream is frozen, rinse off quart-size bag and cut off a corner of the bag. Squeeze ice cream into a paper cup; enjoy! Makes a 1½ cup serving.

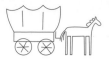

PIONEER DAY

Celebrating Pioneer Day has been a grand tradition in Utah for more than 100 years. Worldwide, more and more members of the Church are beginning to celebrate the faith of their own pioneer ancestors, whether those forebears crossed the plains or joined the Church in recent years. We remember, love, and honor pioneers for their faith, courage, and sacrifice. A well-loved tradition of Pioneer Day is the Days of '47 Parade in downtown Salt Lake City—famous for spectacular floats and enthusiastic spectators.

Some Utahns arise early to grease griddles for pancakes, sausages, and eggs for neighborhood breakfasts. Flag ceremonies, children's parades, pioneer stories, and baseball games are all a happy part of the day. Others enjoy a backyard barbecue or head for a cookout in the mountains, where watermelons stay cold in nearby streams. Some celebrate by cooking up an authentic pioneer meal, like the one that follows, complete with Pioneer Beef Stew, Sourdough Bread, and Plum Cobbler. Whatever your style of celebration, it is heartwarming to reflect on the long pioneer trek, a desert that triumphantly blossomed as a rose (see Isaiah 35:1) and those blessed, honored pioneers (see *Hymns of The Church of Jesus Christ of Latter-day Saints*, no. 36).

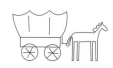

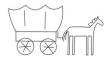

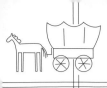

Pioneer Beef Stew

Comfort food for early Mormon pioneers.

1   cup flour
2   tablespoons salt
1   teaspoon pepper
3   pounds round steak
½   cup butter or vegetable oil
6   cups water
2   tablespoons vinegar
2   teaspoons sugar
2   bay leaves
4   carrots, peeled and sliced
4   potatoes, peeled and diced
2   onions, chopped
2   cups chopped tomatoes
2   cloves garlic, minced

Combine flour, salt, and pepper and place on the surface of a cutting board. Place half of round steak on top. With a mallet, pound flour into both sides of meat. Repeat process with other half of meat. Cut meat into bite-sized pieces. In a Dutch oven or other large oven-proof pot, heat butter or oil over medium heat. Add stew meat and brown well. Add water, vinegar, sugar, bay leaves, carrots, potatoes, onions, tomatoes, and garlic. Cover and bake at 325 degrees for 2 hours. Remove covering and cook for an additional hour or until meat is tender and stew is thickened. Makes about 12 cups.

Whole-Wheat Quick Bread

The recipe for this hearty bread came from England with the pioneers. The bread is wonderful served hot with honey butter.

1   egg, beaten
2   cups buttermilk
3   tablespoons molasses or honey
2   tablespoons butter, melted
2   cups whole-wheat flour
1   teaspoon baking soda
1   teaspoon salt
1   teaspoon baking powder

In a bowl, combine egg, buttermilk, molasses or honey, and butter. In a separate bowl, combine flour, baking soda, salt, and baking powder. Stir well; add to first mixture and mix well. Pour into a greased loaf pan. Bake at 400 degrees for about 45 to 50 minutes, until lightly brown. Cool slightly, then turn out of the pan onto a wire rack. Slice while warm. Makes 1 loaf.

Basic Sourdough Batter

Have this batter on hand for whenever you want to make a batch of sourdough bread.

 1   **package dry yeast (1½ teaspoons)**
2½   **cups warm water, divided**
2½   **cups flour**

In a glass or crockery bowl, dissolve yeast in ½ cup of the warm water. Add flour and the remaining 2 cups water and mix well. Cover. Allow to stand at room temperature for 3 to 5 days. Each time Basic Sourdough Batter is used, reserve 1 cup to use as a "starter" for another batch. This may be kept covered in the refrigerator indefinitely. To make it into basic batter again, add 2½ cups flour and 2 cups warm water and allow to stand, covered, at room temperature overnight. It is then ready to use. Remember, one cup should be taken out to use as another "starter."

Sourdough Bread

This good bread was made around pioneer campfires. Serve it hot.

1½   **cups Basic Sourdough Batter (see above)**
 2   **cups lukewarm water**
 ½   **cup sugar**
 1   **tablespoon salt**
 3   **tablespoons butter, melted**
 6   **cups flour**

In a large bowl, combine Basic Sourdough Batter, water, sugar, salt, and butter. Stir together. Gradually stir in flour until dough can be handled. Turn out onto lightly floured board and knead until smooth and elastic, about 5 minutes. Place in a greased bowl and allow to rise about 1 hour. Punch down and allow to rise again for another hour. Divide dough in half and place in 2 well-greased loaf pans. Allow to rise for about 4 hours. Bake at 375 degrees for 40 to 45 minutes, until lightly browned. Cool slightly, then turn onto wire racks. Serve hot. Makes 2 loaves.

Beehive Honey Butter

This is a creamy spread for bread, rolls, or muffins.

 1   **cup honey**
 1   **cup butter, softened**
 1   **teaspoon vanilla**

Combine honey, softened butter, and vanilla. Beat with an electric mixer on high speed for about 3 minutes until thickened. Put into jars and refrigerate. Keeps up to 4 weeks in refrigerator.

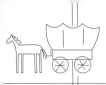

Cabbage Slaw

Early Mormon cooks often served this as a salad or relish. It is excellent served with chicken, beef, or pork.

1   **medium head cabbage, coarsely chopped**
1½ **teaspoons salt**
¾   **cup sugar**
1   **teaspoon celery seeds (optional)**
½   **teaspoon dry mustard**
¾   **cup vinegar**
½   **cup vegetable oil**

Place chopped cabbage in a bowl; set aside. In a small saucepan, combine salt, sugar, celery seeds, mustard, and vinegar. Bring to a boil. Add vegetable oil. Pour over cabbage. Cover and refrigerate for 24 hours. May be kept in refrigerator for several days. Makes about 8 servings.

Rocky Road

You'll be glad you stumbled onto this one.

1   **(14-ounce) can sweetened condensed milk**
2   **(6-ounce) Hershey's® milk chocolate bars with almonds**
1   **(1-ounce) square unsweetened chocolate**
2   **tablespoons butter**
1   **teaspoon vanilla**
¾   **cup toasted pecan halves or almonds**
¾   **cup miniature marshmallows**

In the top of a double boiler, combine sweetened condensed milk, Hershey's chocolate bars, unsweetened chocolate square, and butter. Stir over low heat until melted. Stir in vanilla. Cool for about 15 minutes. Stir in nuts and marshmallows. Pour into a greased 8x8-inch pan. Let cool until firm. Cut into squares. Makes 16 pieces.

Molasses Taffy

After a long day's work, pioneers spent many happy hours singing, dancing, and pulling taffy together. This is old-fashioned fun for all.

1½ **cups light molasses**
¾   **cup sugar**
2   **teaspoons vinegar**
1½ **tablespoons butter**
¼   **teaspoon salt**
    Cornstarch

In a heavy saucepan, combine all ingredients except cornstarch. Stir over medium heat until mixture boils. Continue stirring and boiling until candy reaches the hard-ball stage (244 degrees); remove from heat. Pour onto greased platter or baking sheet. When cool enough to handle, divide into pieces. Pull between greased fingertips until light-colored and stiff. Cut into pieces. Roll in cornstarch so it won't be sticky. Always use caution when heating and working with candy. Eat right away!

Granola

Enjoy along the trail.

- 4 cups quick Quaker® oats
- ¾ cup packed brown sugar
- ½ cup flaked coconut
- ½ cup sliced almonds
- ½ cup pecans or walnuts, coarsely chopped
- ¼ cup water
- ¼ cup vegetable or olive oil
- ¼ cup honey
- ¼ cup peanut butter
- 1 teaspoon vanilla

In a large bowl, mix together oats, brown sugar, coconut, almonds, and pecans or walnuts; set aside. In a saucepan, stir together water, oil, honey, and peanut butter; bring to a boil. Remove from heat; add vanilla and stir honey mixture into oats mixture. Spread on a large greased baking sheet. Bake at 325 degrees for about 45 minutes, stirring occasionally. Makes about 2 pounds.

Plum Cobbler

This old-fashioned favorite is slightly tart.

- ¾ cup packed brown sugar
- 1½ tablespoons cornstarch
- ½ cup water
- 1 teaspoon vanilla

- 4 cups sliced fresh plums
- ½ cup sugar
- 1 tablespoon lemon juice
- 1 tablespoon butter
- 1 recipe Cobbler Topping (see below)
  Ice cream or whipped cream

Combine brown sugar and cornstarch in a large saucepan. Stir in water. Cook and stir over medium heat until thickened and bubbly. Add vanilla. Stir in plums, sugar, lemon juice, and butter; heat through. Pour hot filling into a greased 1½- or 2-quart casserole dish. Keep warm while Cobbler Topping is prepared. Spoon Cobbler Topping over filling, making 6 mounds. Bake at 400 degrees for approximately 20 minutes. Serve with ice cream or whipped cream. Makes 6 servings.

COBBLER TOPPING

- 1 cup flour
- 2 tablespoons sugar
- 1½ teaspoons baking powder
- ¼ teaspoon salt
- ¼ cup butter
- 1 egg, slightly beaten
- ¼ cup milk

Stir together flour, sugar, baking powder, and salt. Cut in butter until mixture resembles coarse crumbs. Combine egg and milk; add all at once to flour mixture. Stir just to moisten.

LABOR DAY WESTERN BARBECUE

There's a bit of nostalgia in the air as Labor Day celebrations get under way. Those gorgeous, carefree summer days are about to end. Fall will soon be arriving, and for some, school will start. What better way to protest than with a good old-fashioned Western barbecue? So get out the cowboy hats, boots, and scarves and get ready for a rip-roarin' good time. Get the bash started with Sheepherder's Dip. Then grill up some Shish Kebabs and enjoy a side of Wild West Rice. Add a few slices of summer watermelon and chow down on Round-Up Rolls. It's just the right season for fabulous homemade Fresh Peach Ice Cream and don't forget to make a batch of crunchy Cowboy Cookies.

You may want to play some old-fashioned games like Run, Sheepy, Run and Kick the Can; or you might enjoy a few gunnysack races. As the evening winds down, sing campfire songs under the stars—even if there's no campfire. "You Are My Sunshine," "Comin' 'Round the Mountain," and "This Land Is Your Land" are all fun favorites. Whatever you do, grab this last chance to celebrate summer.

Sheepherder's Dip

You'll like it, dude!

1 (8-ounce) package cream cheese, softened
1 cup sour cream
1 cup grated cheddar cheese
1 teaspoon Worcestershire sauce
1 (2.5-ounce) package smoked, sliced, pressed beef (lunch meat), chopped
1 cup chopped onion
3 tablespoons butter
1 sheepherder or round loaf bread
Crackers

In a bowl, blend together cream cheese and sour cream. Stir in cheddar cheese, Worcestershire sauce, and smoked beef. In a separate, microwave-safe bowl, combine onions and butter; microwave on high power for 3 minutes. Stir into other ingredients. Cut off top of bread. Scoop out bread. Place mixture in hollowed bread and bake at 350 degrees for about 30 minutes. Serve with bread pieces and crackers.

Shish Kebabs

These are festive and fun for summer.

3 cups vegetable oil
1½ cups soy sauce
1 cup lemon juice
½ cup Worcestershire sauce
2 tablespoons dry mustard
1½ teaspoons chopped fresh parsley or ½ teaspoon dried parsley flakes
2 cloves garlic, minced
6 pounds top sirloin, cut in skewer-size cubes
Assorted vegetables of your choice, such as onions, whole mushrooms, cherry tomatoes, peppers, and zucchini
Rice for 12

In a blender, combine oil, soy sauce, lemon juice, Worcestershire sauce, dry mustard, parsley, and garlic. Blend well and pour over cubed beef. Cover and refrigerate meat for 6 hours or more. When ready to grill, cut vegetables into thick chunks or slices. Thread meat and vegetables on skewers. Broil until meat is cooked through. Serve with rice of your choice. Makes about 12 servings.

Wild West Rice

Rustic and good!

2 (6½-ounce) packages long grain and wild rice
1 medium onion, chopped
1 cup sliced fresh mushrooms
½ cup finely diced celery
¼ cup butter
4 slices bacon, fried crisp, drained, and crumbled
1 (8-ounce) can sliced water chestnuts, drained (optional)

In a saucepan, prepare rice according to package directions; set aside. In a skillet, sauté onion, mushrooms, and celery in butter. Add to rice mixture. Stir in bacon and water chestnuts. Place in a large, well-greased casserole dish. Bake at 350 degrees for about 20 minutes. Makes 10 to 12 servings.

Ranch-Style Beans

You'll love 'em!

1 pound bacon, cut in 2-inch pieces
1 small onion, chopped
1 red or green pepper, chopped
¾ cup packed brown sugar
¼ cup ketchup
¼ cup barbecue sauce
2 tablespoons mustard
2 teaspoons chili powder
2 tablespoons molasses
1 teaspoon salt
1 teaspoon pepper
1 (16-ounce) can white or pinto beans, drained
1 (16-ounce) can lima or butter beans, drained
1 (16-ounce) can red kidney beans, drained
2 (16-ounce) cans pork and beans, undrained

Fry bacon in a large skillet until cooked but not crisp. Add onion and pepper and cook for about 3 minutes. Drain off bacon grease and discard or save for another use. In a large baking dish, combine all other ingredients. Stir in bacon, onion, and pepper mixture. Bake at 325 degrees for about 1 hour. Makes 12 servings.

Round-Up Rolls

They'll come runnin' for these!

- 12 **frozen Rhodes® Cracked Wheat Rolls**
- ¼ **cup butter, melted**
- ¾ **cup freshly grated Parmesan cheese (not packed)**

Place frozen rolls a half-inch apart on a greased baking sheet. Allow to thaw for 30 minutes. Dip tops and sides of rolls in melted butter and then Parmesan cheese. Return to baking sheet. Let rise for 4 hours or until double in size. Bake at 350 degrees for about 30 to 35 minutes. Serve hot. Makes 12 rolls.

Fresh Peach Ice Cream

We all scream for ice cream! Make this irresistible ice cream in a 6-quart ice cream freezer.

- 4 **cups sugar**
- ¼ **teaspoon salt**
- 2 **cups boiling water**
- ¾ **cup orange juice frozen concentrate (undiluted)**
- ¾ **cup lemonade frozen concentrate (undiluted)**
- 2 **cups heavy whipping cream**
- 1 **(12-ounce) can evaporated milk**
- 5 **cups whole milk**
- 3½ **cups peeled and mashed fresh peaches**
  Red and yellow food coloring
- 2 **(7-pound) bags ice**
  Rock salt

In a large pot or bowl, combine sugar, salt, and boiling water. Stir until the sugar is completely dissolved. Add the orange juice and lemonade concentrates. Stir in whipping cream, evaporated milk, whole milk, and peaches. Add a combination of red and yellow food coloring, a drop at a time, to attain the desired peach color. Freeze in a 6-quart freezer, using ice and rock salt according to freezer manufacturer's directions. Makes 5 to 6 quarts.

Cowboy Cookies

These are good, "pardner."

3	cups flour
1	teaspoon baking soda
1	teaspoon baking powder
1	teaspoon cinnamon
1	teaspoon salt
1½	cups butter or margarine, softened
1½	cups sugar
1½	cups packed brown sugar
1	tablespoon vanilla
3	eggs
3	cups chocolate chips
3	cups oats
2	cups flaked coconut
2	cups chopped pecans (optional)

In a bowl, mix flour, baking soda, baking powder, cinnamon, and salt; set aside. In a large bowl, beat butter until smooth and creamy. Gradually beat in sugars and vanilla. Add eggs and beat well. Add flour mixture and stir just until combined. Add chocolate chips, oats, coconut, and pecans. Drop dough by ¼-cup measurements onto greased baking sheet, 3 inches apart. Bake at 350 degrees for about 12 minutes. Makes about 4 dozen large cookies.

AUTUMN

TAILGATE PICNIC

Tailgate picnics aren't just for football games. Consider celebrating your team with a tailgate party at the beginning or ending of the baseball, soccer, or other sports season or as a pre-game festivity for families and fans of local high school rugby players or other athletes. This could also be a way of showing enthusiasm for marathon runners. Families and friends could bring their own picnics and share drinks and desserts. For another menu idea, celebrate your team with a potluck dinner using ideas from the Football Fever Fest section in this book (pages 20–24).

Barbecued Beef Brisket is a great choice for a take-along main dish. Fill a thermos with the barbecued beef, bring along some large buns, and let the team players, athletes, and fans help themselves. Pasta Salad is always a favorite, and Lemon Pudding Fruit Salad will be a tangy and tasty treat for your party-goers. Instead of traditional dips and chips, try the Chocolate Chip Cheese Ball and crackers for a dessert. Snickerdoodles are easy to pack and sure to be a hit. Remember to take along plenty of drinks and ice for the thirsty crowd. Raspberry-Lemonade Slush (see the recipe on page 48) would be a great choice for drinks.

Get into the spirit. Join the fun and celebrate your team!

Barbecued Beef Brisket and Buns

Hear the cheers!

1   4-pound beef brisket (fat removed)

1   (1-ounce) envelope dry onion soup mix

1   (28-ounce) bottle barbecue sauce (K.C. Masterpiece® works well)

1   dozen large buns

Place beef brisket on top of large piece of heavy aluminum foil. Sprinkle onion soup mix over meat. Wrap and seal beef in foil; place in a 9x13-inch baking dish. Bake at 250 degrees for 5 to 6 hours or until tender. Take out of oven. Remove foil and drain off drippings. Cut off excess fat. Place beef brisket on a cutting surface. Slice with the grain as thin as possible. Layer sliced meat and barbecue sauce in a large baking dish. Bake at 250 degrees for an additional 1 to 1½ hours. The meat may be transported in a thermos to keep warm. Fill buns just before serving. Makes 12 sandwichs or 8 main-servings.

Vegetable Basket

Create a basket filled with your favorite vegetables.
Plan for 1 cup of vegetables per person.

Assorted vegetables of your choice, such as zucchini sticks, cherry tomatoes, cauliflower, mushrooms, carrots, celery

1   head romaine or green leaf lettuce

1   head purple-leaf cabbage or red bell pepper, hollowed out to hold dip

Green onions, for garnish

Your favorite dip, such as Spinach Dip (see next page)

Cut up vegetables in desired amounts the night before. Place in plastic bags, add water to crisp, and refrigerate. Before leaving for the picnic, line a basket with foil. Cover with lettuce leaves. Beginning at the back of the basket, cluster vegetables in a colorful array. Place dip in the hollowed-out red pepper or purple cabbage. Overlap long-stemmed green onions and wire them onto basket handle.

Spinach Dip

This is great with vegetables.

1   (10-ounce) package frozen chopped spinach
1   (6-ounce) can sliced water chestnuts (optional)
1   (16-ounce) carton sour cream
1   cup mayonnaise
1   (1-ounce) package ranch dressing mix

Thaw frozen spinach; drain well. Drain and chop water chestnuts. Stir all ingredients together. Chill. Serve with assorted fresh vegetables or crackers.

Potato Salad

A classic!

5   pounds red potatoes
¼   cup diced bell pepper
1   green onion, finely chopped
¼   pound bacon strips, cooked and crumbled
2   cups mayonnaise
1   teaspoon thyme
1   teaspoon salt
1   teaspoon pepper
¼   cup vinegar
¼   cup sugar

In a large saucepan, cover potatoes with water.

Bring water to a boil; cover and reduce heat. Simmer 20 to 25 minutes or until potatoes are just tender. Drain. When cool, cut potatoes into bite-sized pieces. Stir in bell pepper, chopped onion, and bacon. Combine remaining ingredients in a bowl. Pour over potato mixture and stir gently until well coated. Refrigerate until serving time. Makes 12 servings.

Lemon Pudding Fruit Salad

This is a great sidekick.

1   large (20-ounce) can pineapple chunks, drained with juice reserved
1   (15-ounce) can mandarin oranges, drained with juice reserved
1   (3-ounce) package lemon Jell-O®
1   (3-ounce) package lemon pudding (not instant)
1   (8-ounce) tub frozen whipped topping
2   cups fresh strawberries, sliced
2   bananas, sliced
1   cup miniature marshmallows

In a large saucepan, combine reserved fruit juices and enough water to make 3 cups liquid. Bring liquid to a boil. Mix in Jell-O and pudding mix. Cook and stir until thickened. Cool. Stir in whipped topping, fruit, and marshmallows. Refrigerate at least 1 hour. Serve the same day. Makes about 12 servings.

Chocolate Chip Cheese Ball

Take time out to try this fun new idea.

1	(8-ounce) package cream cheese, softened
½	cup butter, softened (no substitutes)
¼	teaspoon vanilla
¾	cup powdered sugar
2	tablespoons packed brown sugar
¾	cup miniature semisweet chocolate chips
¾	cup finely chopped pecans
	Graham crackers or Honey Maid® Chocolate Sticks

In a bowl, beat cream cheese, butter, and vanilla until fluffy. Gradually add sugars. Beat just until combined. Stir in chocolate chips. Cover and refrigerate for 2 hours. Place cream cheese mixture onto a large piece of plastic wrap and shape into a ball. Refrigerate at least 1 hour longer. Roll cheese ball in pecans. Serve with graham crackers or Honey Maid Chocolate Sticks.

Snickerdoodles

These cookies will bring a smile to your face.

1½	cups sugar
1	cup butter or margarine, softened
2	eggs
2¾	cups flour
2	teaspoons cream of tartar
1	teaspoon baking soda
¼	teaspoon salt
¼	cup sugar
2	teaspoons cinnamon

In a bowl, cream together the 1½ cups sugar, butter or margarine, and eggs. In another bowl, stir together flour, cream of tartar, baking soda, and salt. Add to creamed mixture. Shape into 1-inch balls. In a small bowl, mix together the ¼ cup sugar and the cinnamon. Roll balls in sugar-cinnamon mixture. Place 2 inches apart on a greased baking sheet. Bake at 400 degrees for about 8 to 10 minutes. Makes about 4 dozen cookies.

HAPPY BIRTHDAY ITALIAN STYLE

Dazzle someone of any age with a birthday party! To help you start planning, choose a theme and menu the birthday person will love; you might look to the honoree's favorite hobby, sport, color, flower, or food for a theme. Remember to consider whether he or she likes small, low-key events or more festive occasions, such as surprise parties. Once you've decided on an idea, the fun will begin.

The party menu that follows is for someone who loves Italian food. The Lemon Chicken Italiano and Herbed Cheese Bread are melt-in-your-mouth delicious, and the Spinach Gratin and Broiled Tomatoes with Topping are full of color and flavor. Guests will want seconds of the Shrimp and Artichoke Fettuccine, and the Italian Birthday Cake is rich and delicious. A young child's version of the dinner could feature pizza or spaghetti, plain cheese bread, and a fun and festive decorated cake. Add party hats, a birthday chair, bouquets of balloons or flowers, notes in unexpected places, and the sharing of happy memories. Give someone a birthday to remember.

Lemon Chicken Italiano

Celebrate!

- 6 boneless, skinless chicken breasts
- ½ cup flour
- 7 tablespoons butter, divided
- 1 tablespoon olive oil
  Salt and pepper to taste
- 2 cups marinara sauce of your choice
- 4 tablespoons chopped onion
- 2 tablespoons fresh lemon juice
- 2 tablespoons chopped fresh parsley

Pound chicken breasts between sheets of waxed paper or plastic wrap until flattened. Put flour and chicken in a plastic bag and shake to coat chicken. Melt 3 tablespoons of the butter and the 1 tablespoon oil in a large skillet. Place chicken in skillet and cook over medium-high heat for about 5 minutes per side. When cooked through, sprinkle with salt and pepper to taste. Place marinara sauce in the bottom of an oven-proof serving dish; top with chicken. Place chicken in a 250-degree oven to keep warm while preparing the lemon sauce.

To make lemon sauce, melt remaining 4 tablespoons butter in the same skillet, scraping up brown bits from pan. Add onion and sauté until tender. Remove from heat. Add lemon juice and parsley. Pour hot sauce over chicken and serve. Makes 6 servings.

Spinach Gratin

Kids love it, too!

- ¼ cup butter
- 2 cups chopped onion
- ¼ cup flour
- 1 cup cream
- 2 cups milk
- 5 (10-ounce) packages frozen chopped spinach, thawed
- 1½ cups freshly grated Parmesan cheese, divided
- 1 tablespoon salt
- ½ teaspoon pepper

In a large heavy skillet, melt butter over medium heat. Add onions and sauté until tender, about 10 minutes. Add flour. Cook and stir for 2 minutes more. Add cream and milk and cook and stir until thickened. Set aside. Squeeze as much liquid as possible from spinach and add spinach to sauce. Add ½ cup Parmesan cheese and mix well. Stir in salt and pepper. Transfer spinach mixture to baking dish. Sprinkle with remaining Parmesan cheese. Bake at 425 degrees for 20 minutes or until hot and bubbly. May be used as a side dish or as a hot dip with crackers. Makes 8 servings.

Broiled Tomatoes with Topping

Colorful and good.

6   large tomatoes
½   cup white bread crumbs
¼   cup chopped fresh parsley
¼   cup olive oil
2   cloves garlic, minced
1   tablespoon fresh thyme or 1 teaspoon dried
¼   cup freshly grated Parmesan cheese
    Salt and pepper to taste

Cut tomatoes in half; set aside. In a bowl, combine remaining ingredients and stir together. Mound spoonfuls of mixture on top of each tomato. Place on a baking sheet. Broil until lightly browned, about 3 to 4 minutes. Makes 12 servings.

Shrimp and Artichoke Fettuccine

Make someone happy!

8   ounces fettuccine
2   slices bacon, chopped
¼   cup chopped onion
1   cup whipping cream
8   ounces artichoke hearts
½   cup crushed tomatoes
1   teaspoon dried basil leaves
½   teaspoon salt
⅛   teaspoon pepper
½   pound large fresh shrimp
½   cup freshly grated Parmesan cheese

Cook fettuccine according to package directions; drain well and set aside. In a large skillet, cook bacon until cooked through, but not crisp. Add onion and sauté for about 2 minutes. Stir in whipping cream, artichoke hearts, tomatoes, dried basil, salt, and pepper. Heat to a boil, reduce heat, and simmer until artichokes are tender and sauce is thick, about 10 to 15 minutes. Stir shrimp into artichoke mixture. Heat until warmed through and serve over cooked pasta. Top with Parmesan cheese. Makes 4 servings.

Herbed Cheese Bread

Melts in your mouth.

- 1 loaf French bread
- ½ cup butter, softened
- 2 cloves garlic, minced
- 1 teaspoon fresh oregano or ½ teaspoon dried
- 1 teaspoon fresh thyme or ½ teaspoon dried
- 2 cups grated mozzarella cheese

Cut loaf in half lengthwise. Stir butter, garlic, oregano, and thyme together in a small bowl. Spread each half of loaf with herbed butter. Sprinkle 1 cup mozzarella cheese on each half of bread. Broil until cheese is melted. Cut into slices.

Italian Birthday Cake

Light up the party with this dessert.

- 5 eggs, separated
- 2 cups sugar
- 1 cup butter
- 1 tablespoon vanilla
- 1 cup buttermilk
- 2 cups flour
- 1 teaspoon baking soda
- ½ teaspoon salt
- 2 cups coconut
- 1 cup pecans, coarsely chopped
- 1 recipe Cream Frosting
- ½ gallon vanilla ice cream

In a small bowl, beat egg whites with hand mixer for about 3 minutes, or until soft peaks form; set aside. In a separate bowl, cream sugar, butter, and vanilla together. Stir in buttermilk. Beat egg yolks briefly and add to creamed mixture. In a large bowl, stir together flour, baking soda, and salt. Combine creamed mixture with dry mixture, then gently fold in beaten egg whites. Stir in coconut and pecans. Place in greased Bundt pan or 9x13-inch baking dish. Bake at 350 degrees for 30 to 40 minutes. Spread with Cream Cheese Frosting. Serve with a scoop of vanilla ice cream. Makes 12 servings.

CREAM CHEESE FROSTING

- 1 (8-ounce) package cream cheese, softened
- 4 cups powdered sugar
- ¼ cup butter, softened
- 1 tablespoon lemon juice
- 1 teaspoon vanilla

In a bowl, combine ingredients and beat until well blended.

CONFERENCE DINNER

Twice a year, Latter-day Saints all over the world anxiously await the satellite broadcast of general conference. They look forward to hearing inspired messages by beloved leaders and listening to the heavenly sounds of the Mormon Tabernacle Choir.

By preparing simple meals for conference weekend, the focus can be on listening, learning, and feeling the Spirit, rather than on preparing food. Take advantage of this ideal time for conversing, reflecting on messages given, and learning from one another.

The following menu is easy to prepare in advance and can make for a great conference-time dinner. The Missionary Chicken requires little effort and can be counted on. Best Brown Rice is simple, chewy, and crunchy. Enjoy zucchini or a vegetable of your choice in its simple form. Purchase or prepare bread or rolls in advance. The refreshing Raspberry-Banana Salad and gorgeous German Chocolate Cake can also be made in advance.

Weather permitting, consider enjoying your meal on a back porch or table in the yard for a change. Gathering your family together for a Sunday meal is a wonderful tradition worth keeping.

Missionary Chicken

Family and friends will love it!

- 8 boneless, skinless chicken breasts
- 1 teaspoon garlic powder
- 1 teaspoon onion powder
  Salt and pepper to taste
- 2 (10.5-ounce) cans cream of chicken soup
- 2 cups sour cream
- 1 (8-ounce) bag grated Parmesan cheese
- 2 cups sliced mushrooms, sautéed in butter (optional)
- 16 asparagus spears, crisp cooked (optional)

Arrange chicken in a greased 9x13-inch baking dish. Sprinkle evenly with garlic powder, onion powder, and salt and pepper. In a bowl, mix cream of chicken soup and sour cream together. Spread over chicken. Sprinkle with Parmesan cheese. Bake uncovered at 400 degrees for about 45 minutes. Remove from oven. Garnish with mushrooms and asparagus spears, if desired. Makes 8 servings.

Best Brown Rice

Enjoy the chewy texture.

- 2 cups water
- 2 chicken bouillon cubes
- 1 cup brown rice
- 1 tablespoon butter
- 2 (10.3-ounce) boxes chicken-flavored Rice-A-Roni®
  Parsley, mushrooms, slivered almonds or pine nuts, for garnish

Bring water to a boil in a medium saucepan. Add bouillon cubes and simmer until dissolved. In a baking dish, add this mixture to brown rice and butter. Cover and bake at 375 degrees for 1 hour. Remove from oven and let stand covered for 1 hour. Make chicken-flavored Rice-A-Roni according to package directions. Combine brown rice mixture and chicken Rice-A-Roni. Add parsley, mushrooms, slivered almonds or pine nuts in amounts desired. Makes 12 servings.

Zucchini

Enjoy fresh zucchini of the season.

- 6   **medium zucchini**
- 2   **tablespoons butter**
- 1   **teaspoon salt**
- ¼   **teaspoon pepper**
- 1   **cup grated cheddar cheese**

Trim off and discard zucchini ends; cut zucchini into 1-inch slices. In a large saucepan, bring 3 cups of water to a boil. Add zucchini slices. Return to a boil and cover with lid. Reduce heat to medium and cook for 10 minutes. Pour off water and drain well. Place zucchini in a serving dish; add butter. Sprinkle with salt, pepper, and cheese. Makes 8 servings.

Raspberry-Banana Salad

Refreshing!

- 2   **cups water**
- 1   **(6-ounce) package raspberry Jell-O®**
- 1   **(10-ounce) package frozen raspberries with syrup**
- 1   **(20-ounce) can crushed pineapple, undrained**
- 4   **bananas**

Bring water to a boil in a medium saucepan. Add Jell-O and stir until dissolved. Refrigerate until thick and syrupy. Thaw unopened package of raspberries in cold water for about 10 minutes. Carefully add to Jell-O. Stir in crushed pineapple. Dice bananas and add. Pour into a 9x13-inch dish. Let set overnight, if possible, or for several hours. Makes about 12 servings.

German Chocolate Cake

Coconut and pecans make this dessert irresistible.

- 1   **German chocolate cake mix**
- 6   **tablespoons butter**
- ¾   **cup half-and-half**
- 1½ **cups packed brown sugar**
- 1½ **cups flaked coconut**
- 1½ **cups pecans, chopped**
- 1   **teaspoon vanilla extract or ½ teaspoon almond extract**

Prepare cake according to package directions, baking in a greased 9x13-inch pan. In a saucepan, melt butter over medium heat. Stir in half-and-half and brown sugar. Cook and stir until smooth. Add coconut, nuts, and extract. Cool slightly and spread over cooled cake. Makes about 12 servings.

HALLOWEEN

Halloween can be frightfully fun. Children dressed as witches, scarecrows, princesses, and goblins happily march in school parades. Pumpkins, cornstalks, and bales of hay decorate lighted porches. Licorice, candy corn, and gummy worms decorate cupcakes; and witches' brew is served from a steaming cauldron.

If you're planning a party, make sure food is part of the fun. Bring jack-o-lantern cakes, pumpkin-and-ghost sandwiches with olive faces, and orange Jell-O to the table. Two wonderful main dishes to choose from are Taco Salad or Sloppy Joes in a Pumpkin. Peanut Butter Witches' Fingers, Chocolate-Covered Spiders, and Monster Cookies are frightfully delicious. Hollowed-out oranges make great little "pumpkins" in which to serve Jell-O or orange sherbet.

Perhaps you'd like to plan a festive family or neighborhood activity complete with scary music, games, a parade, doughnuts and cider, and surprises. Have fun!

Taco Salad

This is piles of fun to stack and eat.

- 2 pounds ground beef
- 2 (1.25-ounce) packages taco seasoning mix
- 1½ cups water
- 1 avocado
  Juice from 1 lime
- 1 head lettuce, shredded
- 1 (15-ounce) can red kidney beans, drained
- 4 tomatoes, chopped
- 2 cups grated cheddar cheese
- 1 (10-ounce) package Fritos® corn chips or 6 flour tortillas
- 1 recipe Cilantro-Lime Dressing (see next column)

Brown ground beef in a large skillet. Stir in taco seasoning mixes and water. Simmer, stirring occasionally, for about 15 minutes or until water is absorbed. Chop avocado. Squeeze juice of lime over chopped avocado; carefully stir to coat. Place ground beef, avocado, lettuce, kidney beans, tomatoes, cheddar cheese, and corn chips in separate bowls. Let each person make their own salad beginning with corn chips on a plate. Or, if using tortillas, brush each side with oil and briefly cook in a skillet until lightly browned on each side. Place the tortilla in a large individual bowl. Top with other ingredients and desired amount of Cilantro-Lime Dressing. Makes 6 servings.

CILANTRO-LIME DRESSING

- 1 (1-ounce) packet ranch dressing mix
- 1 cup mayonnaise
- 1 cup sour cream
- 1 (3-inch) jalapeño pepper, cut and seeded
- 2 tablespoons chopped onion
- ⅓ cup chopped cilantro
  Juice of 1 lime

Blend all ingredients in blender.

Mandarin Orange Jell-O Salad

Kids of all ages will ask for more!

- 1 cup water
- 1 large (6-ounce) package orange Jell-O®
- 2 cups orange juice
- 1 (15-ounce) can mandarin oranges, drained
- 1 cup whipping cream, plus sugar to sweeten

In a saucepan, bring water to a boil. Add Jell-O and stir until dissolved. Stir in orange juice; refrigerate until syrupy. Stir in mandarin oranges. Pour into an 8x8-inch dish or large pie plate. Refrigerate several hours until set. Whip and sweeten cream; spread over top. Makes about 8 servings.

Sloppy Joes in a Pumpkin

Surround pumpkin with autumn leaves for a centerpiece.

3	pounds ground beef
1	teaspoon salt
1	cup chopped onion
1	cup ketchup
1	(10-ounce) can tomato soup
2	tablespoons vinegar
2	tablespoons Worcestershire sauce
2	tablespoons packed brown sugar
1	small to medium hollowed-out pumpkin
12	hamburger buns

Brown ground beef in a large skillet; drain fat. Sprinkle with salt. Add chopped onion and cook until tender. Stir in ketchup, tomato soup, vinegar, Worcestershire sauce, and brown sugar. Simmer for 30 minutes. Carve and clean out a pumpkin of desired size. Place on a baking sheet in a 325-degree oven. Warm pumpkin for about 30 minutes. Remove from oven and spoon in sloppy Joe mixture, using the pumpkin as a serving container. Spoon into hamburger buns to serve. Makes 12 servings.

Frog's Eye Salad

You won't croak!

1	cup acini de pepe pasta
1	(20-ounce) can pineapple tidbits, juice reserved
1	(20-ounce) can crushed pineapple
2	(15-ounce) cans mandarin oranges, drained
1	(12-ounce) tub frozen whipped topping, thawed
2	cups miniature marshmallows
1	cup flaked coconut (optional)
½	cup chopped maraschino cherries (optional)
	Green food coloring

Cook pasta according to package directions; drain well and set aside to cool. Pour reserved pineapple juice over pasta. Add pineapple tidbits, crushed pineapple, mandarin oranges, whipped topping, and marshmallows. Stir in coconut and cherries, if desired. Stir in green food coloring, one drop at a time, to desired color. Place in refrigerator overnight. Makes about 12 servings.

Monkey Bread

They'll "hang around" for more.

- 20 frozen Rhodes® or other brand rolls
- ¾ cup sugar, white or brown
- 1 tablespoon cinnamon
- ½ cup butter, melted

Thaw 20 frozen rolls by placing ten at a time on a plate in the microwave. Set microwave on defrost setting or lowest setting. Microwave the rolls at one-minute intervals for three minutes, turning the plate after each minute. Remove from microwave. Cut each roll in half. Stir together sugar and cinnamon. Dip each roll in melted butter, then roll in sugar-cinnamon mixture. Layer rolls in a greased Bundt pan. Pour any remaining butter or sugar-cinnamon mixture over top of rolls. Allow rolls to rise till double in volume, about three hours. Bake at 350 degrees for about 25 minutes. Turn pan upside down onto serving plate. Serve immediately. Makes 8 to 10 servings.

Little Apple Dippers

Fun to make on a frightful night.

- 1 (14-ounce) package caramels
- 10 small apples (Jonathans work well)
- 10 Popsicle sticks
- 1 cup miniature marshmallows
- 1 tablespoon water
- 1 cup toffee bits, granola, chopped nuts, or chocolate sprinkles

Let children unwrap caramels. Lightly grease a foil-lined baking sheet. Rinse and dry apples. Insert Popsicle stick into stem end of each apple. In a bowl, place caramels, marshmallows, and water. Microwave on high power for 1 minute. Stir. Microwave for 1 minute more. Stir until smooth. Dip bottom half of apples in caramel and then in topping of your choice. Place on foil-lined baking sheet. Makes 10 caramel apples.

Peanut Butter Witches' Fingers

"Try these, my pretty."

- ½ **cup butter**
- ½ **cup sugar**
- ½ **cup packed brown sugar**
- 1 **egg**
- ½ **cup peanut butter**
- 1 **teaspoon vanilla**
- 1 **cup flour**
- 1 **cup quick Quaker® Oats**
- ½ **teaspoon baking soda**
- 1 **(11-ounce) bag chocolate chips**
- ½ **cup powdered sugar**
- ¼ **cup peanut butter**
- 2 **tablespoons evaporated milk**

In a bowl, cream together butter, sugar, brown sugar, egg, ½ cup peanut butter, and vanilla. Set aside. In a separate bowl, stir together flour, quick Quaker® Oats, and baking soda; add to creamed mixture and beat together until well blended. Spread in a greased 9x13-inch pan. Bake at 350 degrees for about 20 minutes. Remove from oven. Immediately sprinkle with chocolate chips. Spread with a knife to cover surface. In a bowl, combine powdered sugar, ¼ cup peanut butter, and evaporated milk. Spread over the bars in a swirling motion. Allow to cool and cut into fingers. Makes about 16.

Chocolate-Covered Spiders

Creepy, crawly, and good.

- 1 **cup chocolate chips**
- 1 **cup butterscotch or peanut butter chips**
- 1 **(3-ounce) can chow mein noodles**
- 1 **cup salted Spanish or cocktail peanuts**

In a large saucepan, combine chips and cook over low heat until melted, stirring constantly. Add chow mein noodles and peanuts. Stir until both are well coated with chocolate mixture. Drop spoonfuls of the mixture onto a greased, foil-lined baking sheet and refrigerate until hard, about 30 minutes. Vary the size of your spoonfuls to get spiders of varying sizes.

Amazing Low-Fat Pumpkin Cookies

Delicious cookies made in minutes.

- 1 **spice cake mix**
- 1 **(29-ounce) can pumpkin**
- 1 **(11-ounce) bag chocolate chips (optional)**

In a bowl, mix together cake mix and pumpkin. Add chocolate chips if desired. Drop by tablespoons onto greased baking sheet, about 1 inch apart. Bake at 400 degrees for about 20 minutes. Makes about 4 dozen.

Monster Cookies

Don't be scared—you'll like them.

- 1½ cups butter or margarine
- 2 cups sugar
- 2½ cups packed brown sugar
- 6 eggs
- 1 (28-ounce) jar peanut butter
- 2 tablespoons light corn syrup
- 4 teaspoons baking soda
- 2 teaspoons vanilla
- 9 cups oats
- 1 (14-ounce) package M&M's®

In a large bowl, cream together butter or margarine, sugar, and brown sugar. Mix in eggs, peanut butter, corn syrup, baking soda, vanilla, and oats. Stir in M&M's. With an ice cream scoop, drop batter on a greased baking sheet. Bake at 350 degrees for 10 to 12 minutes. Cool for 5 minutes before removing from baking sheet. Makes about 4 dozen large cookies.

Grandchildren's Popcorn

With a little help, kids can make these.

- 1 bag microwave popcorn
- ½ cup butter
- ½ (10.5-ounce) bag miniature marshmallows

Pop popcorn in the microwave; set aside. With a grown-up's help, melt butter in a large saucepan over low heat. Add marshmallows; stir until melted. Remove from heat. Add popped popcorn and stir until coated. Spread out on a piece of waxed paper to cool. You can also form into popcorn balls. Then eat 'em up . . . YUM!

GIVING THANKS

One of the most cherished days of the year is Thanksgiving. And finding a few hours for preparing during the weeks before Thanksgiving will make this day joyful for everyone, including you. Let the whole family help with planning. Give out assignments early for getting the home ready. Someone can gather branches, berries, gourds, and dried foliage for making centerpieces. Others can help by making place cards; decorating napkins; helping with a program; rounding up books, games, and toys to keep children entertained; and setting tables. Several foods can be made days in advance, such as Golden Squash Soup, Jellied Cranberry Sauce, and Feather-Light Overnight Rolls (see page 42).

In addition to a grand meal, other unique Thanksgiving traditions abound. One favorite is retelling "The Legend of the Five Kernels." To do this at your house, place five kernels of corn or candy by each plate at the dinner table. Before the meal begins, have someone tell the following story:

"It was very cold for the Pilgrims that first winter. Food was in short supply. Some days, they had only five kernels of corn. When spring came, the Pilgrims planted the remaining corn. The sun and rain helped the seed to grow, and much food was harvested in the fall. Every Thanksgiving thereafter, the Pilgrims placed five kernels of corn beside each plate to remind them of their blessings:

"The first kernel reminded them of the autumn beauty.

"The second reminded them of their love for each other.

"The third reminded them of their family's love.

"The fourth reminded them of their friends, especially their Indian brothers.

"The fifth kernel reminded them of their freedom."

Enjoy your feast; and in the spirit of the season, remember to "live in thanksgiving daily, for the many mercies and blessings which [the Lord] doth bestow upon you" (Alma 34:38).

ROASTING A TURKEY TO PERFECTION

Your first decision will be whether to select a fresh or frozen turkey. A fresh bird is more expensive but will save time and valuable refrigerator space. Purchase the fresh bird the day before you want to roast it, but remember to reserve your turkey in advance with the butcher. A frozen turkey needs to be defrosted. The preferred method is to defrost in the refrigerator. Allow one day of thawing for every five pounds. For example, a fifteen-pound turkey will require three days to defrost thoroughly.

Now you are ready to prepare the turkey for roasting.

1. Remove the giblets.

2. Rinse the bird inside and out with water.

3. Pat dry with paper towels.

4. If you are stuffing the bird, do so now with freshly prepared dressing. If using previously frozen stuffing, allow time for stuffing to thaw overnight in the refrigerator. Never stuff turkey ahead of time; wait until you are ready to roast the turkey. Stuff loosely, allowing about ¾ cup stuffing per pound of bird. Don't forget to stuff the neck cavity.

Once stuffed, pull the neck skin up and pin it down with a skewer to enclose the opening. Also skewer the body cavity opening to protect stuffing or place a piece of tin foil over the opening. (Any extra stuffing should be placed in a buttered casserole dish and baked at 350 degrees for about 30 minutes.)

5. Brush the skin with melted butter or oil.

6. Tuck the drumsticks under the folds of skin or tie together with string.

7. Nowadays, many turkeys come with built-in thermometers. If not, insert a meat thermometer into the thickest part of the thigh. The thermometer should point towards the body and should not touch the bone.

8. Place the bird on a rack in a roasting pan preheated to 350 degrees. Cover with an open-sided foil tent that does not touch the bird and allows the air to circulate. During the last 45 minutes of baking, remove the foil tent if more browning is desired. Basting is not necessary, but will promote even browning. The turkey is done when the thigh meat reaches an internal temperature of 180 degrees. The stuffing temperature should be at least 165 degrees.

9. When the turkey is done, remove it from the oven and allow it to stand for 30 minutes to retain juices.

10. Serve the stuffing by removing it from the turkey and placing it in a serving bowl. Never let stuffing sit in a turkey once it is finished cooking. Remove the stuffing immediately and serve or refrigerate.

11. Before you begin carving, have a warm serving platter ready and waiting.

Weight of Bird	Roasting Time (Unstuffed)	Roasting Time (Stuffed)
10 to 18 pounds	3 to 3½ hours	3¾ to 4½ hours
18 to 22 pounds	3½ to 4 hours	4½ to 5 hours
22 to 24 pounds	4 to 4½ hours	5 to 5½ hours
24 to 29 pounds	4½ to 5 hours	5½ to 6¼ hours

Golden Squash Soup

It's good and good for you.

2 apples
2½ pounds banana squash (1 large piece)
1 cup chicken broth
2 tablespoons butter
1½ cups chopped onion
2 teaspoons salt
¼ teaspoon pepper
2 teaspoons mild curry powder (optional)
1 cup apple juice
1 cup cream
Salt to taste

Peel, core, and cut apples in half. Place apples and squash face-down on greased baking sheet. Bake at 350 degrees for 1 hour. Scoop out squash. Place squash, apples, and chicken broth in a blender and mix until well blended; set aside. In a large cooking pot, melt butter over low heat. Add onions and cook for about 5 minutes. Stir occasionally. Add salt, pepper, and curry powder and stir together. Add apple juice, cream, and squash mixture. Stir and heat through. Do not boil. Salt to taste. Serve hot. Makes about 8 cups.

Savory Sausage Stuffing

This is certain to become a star of your feast.

¾ cup butter, melted
½ cup chopped onions
1 cup finely diced celery
1 (8 ounce) can mushrooms, undrained
12 cups bread, broken into small pieces
½ pound ground sausage, cooked and drained
¾ teaspoon salt
½ teaspoon pepper
2 tablespoons finely chopped fresh sage or 2 teaspoons dried sage
2 apples, peeled, cored, and grated (optional)

Sauté onions and celery in melted butter until tender. Add undrained mushrooms. Combine mixture with bread. Add sausage and stir. Sprinkle evenly with salt, pepper, and sage. Add grated apples if desired. Do not stuff dressing into turkey until ready to bake. Dressing can be frozen ahead. Thaw one day in advance in refrigerator. If not stuffing turkey, bake stuffing in a buttered casserole at 350 degrees for 30 minutes. Makes 6 servings.

Jellied Cranberry Sauce

The tart cranberry flavor will enhance turkey and stuffing.

1   **cup sugar**

1   **cup water**

1   **package (12-ounce) fresh or frozen cranberries**

Combine sugar and water in a medium saucepan and stir to dissolve sugar. Bring to a boil; add cranberries and return to a boil. Reduce heat. Boil gently about 10 minutes, stirring occasionally. Remove from heat. Before cooling, place a wire mesh strainer over a mixing bowl. Pour contents of saucepan into strainer. Mash cranberries with the back of a spoon, frequently scraping the outside of the strainer, until no pulp is left. Stir contents of bowl. Pour into serving container. Cover and cool at room temperature. Can be made several days in advance and refrigerated, or several weeks ahead and frozen. Makes about 2 cups.

Classic Mashed Potatoes

Everyone loves them!

5   **pounds russet potatoes**

½   **cup butter, softened**

1½ **cups milk or cream**

    Salt and pepper to taste

Peel potatoes and cut into large chunks. Place in a large cooking pot. Add water to cover. Bring to a boil over medium heat and cook until potatoes are very tender, about 40 minutes. Drain water. Place the pan over low heat. With a potato masher, thoroughly mash the potatoes. Add butter and milk or cream. Mix together. Add salt and pepper to taste. Makes 8 servings.

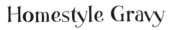

Homestyle Gravy

Gravy becomes lumpy when flour particles become stuck together. This can be avoided by cooking together equal parts flour and fat (butter or vegetable oil). This mixture is known as a roux *and serves as a thickener for gravy.*

½ **cup flour**

½ **cup butter or vegetable oil**

4 **cups chicken broth**

½ **cup water**

Drippings from turkey

Salt and pepper to taste

To make roux, whisk together flour and butter or vegetable oil in a heavy pan. Cook over medium heat, stirring constantly until all flour particles are blended. Stir in chicken broth. Simmer over medium heat, stirring frequently, for about 5 minutes until well blended.

After removing the cooked turkey, deglaze the roasting pan by placing it over medium heat and adding ½ cup water. Stir constantly and scrape the bottom of the pan to loosen browned bits. Simmer for 1 minute.

Pour the glaze from the roasting pan into the gravy base (the roux and broth mixture), stirring constantly. Cook until mixture boils and thickens, about 5 to 8 minutes. Season to taste with salt and pepper.

Serve hot with mashed potatoes, stuffing, and turkey. Have extra turkey-gravy-mix packets on hand if more gravy is needed. Makes 4 cups savory gravy.

Creamed Corn

Corn reminds us of the first Thanksgiving.

4 **(15-ounce) cans corn**

1 **cup sour cream**

½ **teaspoon salt**

2 **tablespoons butter**

In a large saucepan, warm corn over medium heat. Just before serving, drain off liquid. Reduce heat to low and stir in sour cream, salt, and butter. Makes 12 servings.

Green Beans with Browned Butter

These beans are "all dressed up."

3   (9-ounce) packages frozen cut green
    beans
¼   cup butter
¼   cup slivered almonds or pine nuts
    Salt to taste

In a large saucepan, bring 2 cups water to a boil. Add beans. Cover and return to a boil. Reduce heat and simmer for about 10 minutes or until beans are tender. Pour water off and set aside. In a separate pan, melt butter over low heat. Add almonds or pine nuts. Stir constantly until butter and nuts are lightly browned. Pour mixture over beans. Toss to coat. Salt to taste. Keep warm over low heat until ready to serve. Makes 8 servings.

Baked Apples

A sweet and spicy side dish.

6   apples (Rome beauties work well)
¼   cup cranberries
¼   cup walnuts
¼   cup packed brown sugar
¼   cup bread crumbs
1   teaspoon cinnamon
    Zest of 1 lemon
3   tablespoons butter, melted

Core apples. Remove a ½-inch slice from the bottom of the apples so they will sit flat in a pan. Place in a greased baking dish and set aside. In a bowl, combine remaining ingredients. Stuff apples with mixture. Bake, covered with foil, at 375 degrees for about 25 minutes or until filling is cooked and bubbly. Makes 6 servings.

Candied Yams

These are a sweet tradition.

5 pounds yams or sweet potatoes (about 6 large)
¼ cup butter
½ cup packed brown sugar
Salt and pepper to taste
2 cups miniature marshmallows
½ cup orange juice

Peel yams or sweet potatoes and cut into slices about ½-inch thick. In a greased 9x13-inch baking dish, arrange yam slices, overlapping them as you go. Cut butter into small pieces. Sprinkle butter pieces and brown sugar evenly over yams. Season lightly with salt and pepper. Place foil tightly over yams. Bake at 325 degrees for about 25 minutes. Remove from oven. Uncover dish. Scatter marshmallows over the yams. Drizzle orange juice over top. Return dish to the oven and continue baking, basting occasionally, until marshmallows are melted and gooey, about 15 to 20 minutes. Makes 8 to 10 servings.

Pecan Pie

A grand Thanksgiving favorite.

⅓ cup butter, softened
1 cup packed brown sugar
1 cup light corn syrup
¼ teaspoon salt
3 eggs, lightly beaten
1 teaspoon vanilla
1 9-inch pie shell, unbaked
1 cup pecan halves
Whipped cream or ice cream, as desired

In a medium bowl, cream butter and brown sugar together. Add corn syrup, salt, eggs, and vanilla; beat well. Pour into a 9-inch unbaked pie shell. Sprinkle pecans over top. Place on a baking sheet. Bake at 350 degrees for approximately 45 minutes, just until center is set. Cool and top with whipped cream or ice cream. Makes 6 servings.

Pumpkin Pie Squares

Everyone in your family will be thankful you made this tasty treat.

- 1 **cup flour**
- ½ **cup butter or margarine, softened**
- ½ **cup quick Quaker® Oats**
- 1 **cup packed brown sugar, divided**
- 4 **cups pumpkin**
- 2 **(12-ounce) cans evaporated milk**
- 4 **eggs**
- 1½ **cups sugar**
- 2 **teaspoons cinnamon**
- ¼ **teaspoon ground cloves**
- 1 **teaspoon nutmeg**
- 2 **tablespoons butter, chilled**
- 1 **cup pecans, chopped**
- ½ **pint whipping cream**

For crust, combine flour, ½ cup softened butter or margarine, quick Quaker® Oats, and ½ cup of the brown sugar. Mix well and pat into a greased 9x13-inch baking dish. Bake at 350 degrees for about 10 minutes. Cool.

While crust is baking and cooling, combine pumpkin, evaporated milk, eggs, sugar, cinnamon, cloves, and nutmeg. Beat well and pour over cooled crust.

Make a crumble topping by cutting 2 tablespoons chilled butter into the remaining ½ cup brown sugar. Stir in pecans and sprinkle over pumpkin filling. Bake at 350 degrees for about 50 minutes. Whip cream and serve a dollop on each pumpkin pie square. Makes about 12 servings.

Cranberry Sherbet

A refreshing alternative to rich desserts.

- 2 **cups (½ pound) fresh cranberries**
- 1½ **cups water**
- 1 **cup sugar**
- 1½ **teaspoons unflavored gelatin**
- ¼ **cup cold water**
- **Juice of 1 lemon**

In a saucepan, cook cranberries in 1½ cups water over medium heat until skins pop. Press through sieve or strainer. Add sugar and stir until dissolved. Soften gelatin in cold water, about 5 minutes. Add to warm cranberry puree and stir. Cool. Stir in lemon juice. Place mixture in a container and freeze until firm. Break into chunks. Beat smooth with electric beater. Return quickly to freezer. Freeze until firm. Makes 4 servings.